THIS TEACHING LIFE
A memoir of schooldays in Ireland

Tom McElligott

THE LILLIPUT PRESS

First published in 1986 by
THE LILLIPUT PRESS LTD
Gigginstown, Mullingar, Co. Westmeath, Ireland

British Library Cataloguing in Publication Data
McElligott, T. J.
This teaching life: a memoir of schooldays in Ireland
1. High school teaching — Ireland
I. Title
373.11'02'0924 LA646

ISBN 0-946640-14-9

Cover design: Jarlath Hayes
Cover illustration: 'The Country Schoolmaster'
by Nathaniel Grogan (d. 1807)
courtesy of the British Museum and
The Cork Historical & Archæological Society Journal

Set in 11 on 14 Garamond by
Redsetter Ltd. of Dublin
and printed in England by
Richard Clay (The Chaucer Press) Ltd.
of Bungay, Suffolk

ACKNOWLEDGMENTS

This is not in any sense a formal study of the life led by a secondary teacher. Rather is it intended to be a discursive narrative of some of the events marking such a life.

I owe a debt of gratitude to many to whom I had written or who, in conversation, suggested matter for inclusion. I wish in particular to thank Mr Michael Hewson, Director of the National Library, and his staff; Mrs Helen Kilclyne, Roscommon County Librarian; Brother Felin Burns, Superior-General, De La Salle order; Oliver Marshall, Librarian, Department of Education; Father S. Clyne, Principal, St Patrick's College; Dr John Coolahan, University College, Dublin; Dr Brendan Kennelly, Trinity College, Dublin; Mr Conall Cannon, Headmaster, Sandymount High School; Con Burns, N.T.; Brother Patrick Hederman, O.S.B.; Rev. P. Skelly, O.P.; Terence de Vere White.

CONTENTS

ONE

Cork: Early Days and University

ANYONE LIVING IN CORK in the years before 1921 must have some memories of the British occupation. I can recall only curfew, the most serious aspect of which, for those of us who were very young at the time, was that all hurling on the road had to end on summer evenings by 8 p.m. My parents had passes issued by the British military permitting them to use the Gaol Walk which led from the Western Road to where we lived on Highfield Avenue. I found it dangerously exciting when, clutching the hands of my parents, I heard the challenge of a sentry ring out 'Who goes there?' to be answered by a reassuring voice, 'Friend'.

My parents grew up not too far from one another in north Kerry. My mother was born in Rathmore and my father in Listowel. Almost thirty years were to pass before they met and then it was in Cork city where my father was in the RIC and stationed at Union Quay. He resigned on the occasion of his marriage in 1910 and by the time that I came into the world he had been working as an accountant with Messrs Sutton on the South Mall for some years.

Among my earliest memories is that of waiting for him while sheltering in a doorway on the Mall with my mother.

It must have been near closing time in the office when a lorry with Auxiliaries pulled out of Pembroke Street and stopped almost opposite us. The 'Auxies' jumped down, took the whips from the jarveys who had a stand near Parnell Bridge and began to drive the passers-by off the street.

There may have been sharp political divisions within the circle of my relations, but of these I knew nothing. They have little meaning for young children. However, I do know that I was frightened when I saw a cousin get up, genuflect and walk boldly out of the Lough chapel in protest when Father Pat O'Toole prayed for an RIC man who had been shot dead on the steps of the Catholic church in Bandon.

Only once did I see someone being 'lifted' by British soldiers. It was night-time and I had crept into my parents' bedroom which was in the front of the house when I heard a lorry stopping almost at our gate. Peering through the uplifted blind, I saw a man named Doran being taken away under armed escort.

When the British withdrew and when curfew ended I was able to fulfil an early ambition and become an altar boy. This meant rising at 6.30 a.m. to serve 7 o'clock Mass for Father O'Connell, who was chaplain to the Bon Secours Convent. Father O'Connell was extremely deaf and on one occasion after I had stolen a goldfish from a pond in the grounds, I decided to confess my crime to him while he was vesting in the sacristy. His reply was somewhat unexpected. 'Go and take a few aspirins,' he said in kindly fashion. I was taken aback but thought it well not to pursue the matter, satisfied that even if he had misunderstood the nature of the offence, I was cleared of my sin.

When the time came to make my first communion I had the unwanted distinction of making it alone. I had fallen from the back of a milk-car a few days before my class at Glasheen national school made theirs. Great was my shame when a fortnight later I was included with the 'first-communioners' of a neighbouring girls' school, all fluffy in white organdie. For my photograph on that occasion I was brought, as was almost every child in Cork, to Leopold's Studio in Patrick Street. I was taken clutching a prayerbook and smiling seraphically against a background of palms, which it was assumed would display me to best advantage.

Earlier photographs, all of which I think I have destroyed, showed me complete with bucket, spade, floppy hat and, horror of horrors, wearing a pinafore! My first suit was made for me by a tailor named Murphy who lived in Parkowen off Quaker Road. He was warned by my mother to 'make it big enough for him', and he did.

Socks in those days were always carefully darned and shoes had Blakey's protectors on toecaps and heels as well as 'taobhíní' on the sides. Newly soled shoes were rubbed with a nutmeg grater to ensure that the wearer remained vertical, and we were admonished by our parents to use a shoehorn so as not to break their backs. 'Planned obsolescence' was a phrase yet unborn.

Family walks, so very much a part of most children's Sunday at that time, have now given way to family drives. My first walks were on the Model Farm Road as far as Cáit Shea's Lane. Later, after we had moved to the North Main Street, the route changed. Seán Ó Faoláin in his autobiography *Vive Moi!* gives a realistic picture of such walks. For him, as for me and my sister, there was a choice of two or three itineraries. 'St Luke's' might offer the attraction of some stills of Mary Pickford and Clara Bow in the Palace or Coliseum Cinema. 'Sunday's Well' could possibly show us mullet feeding on sewage or a flotilla of swans near Wellington Bridge. We considered the Lower Glanmire Road very dull until 'the Fisheries' was reached and we could look forward to the possibility of seeing a racing eight swamped by the wash from the sea-going *Innisfallen*.

I preferred the road leading up towards St Luke's. It was then, and has remained, a determinedly private area, full of 'secret gardens' into which people seem to have withdrawn out of sight of the city at their feet. Solid pillars and looped chains on garden railings proclaim the intense privacy of each householder and a determination to resist intrusion and change. Where else in the Republic will you find so many names redolent of another age – Empress Place, Clarence Villas, Grosvenor Terrace, Wellington Road! Rebel Cork seems far away.

Outings to the seaside were for most of us either to Crosshaven or Youghal. My mother remembered going to Crosshaven by the Green Boat, but apart from one journey by wagonette I can only remember going there by train and then toiling up what appeared to be endless hills to the bays. Nice social distinctions were observed in one's choice of bay. Graball Bay, would you not guess from the appalling name, was very down market and the status of Church Bay uncertain. Noblett's and Myrtleville were the local equivalents of the then much favoured Deauville and Trouville. It would be unfair to the memory of the two presiding deities at the Corporation Baths in Cork city, Bob and Bill, to say that I learned to swim at Noblett's because they had ensured that I had mastered 'the dog's paddle' before ever I committed myself to the Atlantic.

Most of the sporting activities of those days were free and only team games were organized. You may not have kept a beagle for the drag-hunt or a pigeon for racing, but you could be sure that in most houses there was a hurley and, in many, a pair of iron bowls. Sunday was a day when, after an early Mass, the young people in a house were off in pursuit of a variety of pastimes. Among the early risers were bird-catchers, usually seen carrying a cage in which there was a goldfinch or a bullfinch as a decoy. The cage was hung on a tree and when a bird landed on the cage roof, a trap tipped it in. Racing-pigeons were usually timed to arrive back at their loft on a Sunday morning and as I associated this sport almost entirely with the North parish, I never knew the thrill of being 'a watcher of the skies'. Bowl-playing was, however, popular North and South of the river and it also crossed the social divides so that it was not unusual for a university professor and a workman on the grounds to go for 'a score' up Dublin Hill or out Waterfall.

At a time when enclosed pitches were still few, I remember holding on to the ropes as the crowd swayed on to the field when Blackrock and St Finbarr's played in the big field below the African Missionary Church at Wilton. Half a mile away, in Long's at Victoria Cross, I saw the great Fordson soccer team of 1926 play Bray Unknowns, and I think that I could still name that eleven who brought the Free State Cup to Cork.

How long ago it all seems may be judged from the carefree manner in which the grounds secretary, Captain Lalor, collected the gate-money after a match on the Mardyke. He simply went along unaccompanied to each turnstile, put the takings in his Gladstone bag and walked home! Players arrived by side-car or on foot. There was the odd occasion when the huge laundry-basket containing the players' togs was used to conceal some prominent figure in the Gaelic Athletic Association whose presence at either a rugby or a soccer match would have contravened the infamous 'foreign games' rule.*

It must not be thought from the foregoing that in my home sport was encouraged to the detriment of the Arts. I was brought to hear the Warblers at the Father O'Leary Total Abstinence Hall on Bandon Road almost as soon as I could walk. From that to theatre-going at the Opera House was an easy transition. Whether in the pit or in the back stalls, both favoured by my mother, I watched impatiently for the first tremor of the great curtain that was to unfold upon a world of magic. By 1932, when the Savoy Cinema was opened, I was old enough to set off alone for that Temple of Venus where many solid grandfathers of today sang songs of love to the sound of Sidney Bridgeman at the organ.

Open-air theatre was known to the citizens of Cork long before Londoners enjoyed it in Regent's Park. The Cork Shakespearian Company presented *A Midsummer Night's Dream* in the quadrangle of the University College during that glorious summer of 1921 when, against the backdrop of trees overlooking the old quarry, we imagined ourselves in the Staffordshire countryside,

> Where oxlips and the nodding violet grows,
> Quite over-canopied with luscious woodbine,
> With sweet musk-roses and with eglantine.

When I left school in Glasheen I was sent to Presentation College on the Western Road. It was a school in which

---

*The Congress of the Association in 1970 abolished the rule.

the teachers believed in the efficiency of the cane, total obedience and learning by rote. So it is that to this day I can, without too much trouble, recite the Latin prepositions that prefer to be followed by accusative case, such as *ante, apud, ad, adversus, circum, circa, citra, cis.* Nor is it beyond my powers of recall to recite the tricky little stanza which lists the verbs that have a liking for the dative case. It runs as follows: 'A dative put with show and give, tell, envy, spare, permit, believe, obey, command; to these add threaten, succour, pardon, please, with *vacare*, *displicere*, feel, favour, hurt, resist and *indulgere*.'

Nor must it be thought that my acquaintance with Latin was confined to the rules of grammar. I can also, if ever called upon, give a fair translation into English of extracts from Virgil's *Aeneid*, particularly those extracts from the texts listed for the Matriculation of 1931. Kelly's *Key to the Classics* made it almost superfluous to possess the original. Once given the vital opening line, anyone in my class could have translated the beautiful lines which begin with the words, 'I am not such as I was under the reign of the good Cynarus. Spare, O mother of the soft Cupids, to bend to thy harsh requests one already hardened on the verge of forty years.'

Latin was not the only subject which was taught effectively at Presentation College, Cork, in the late 'twenties. It had a strong mathematical tradition and so we learned algebraic formulae and geometrical theorems, wrote '*Ad maiorem Dei gloriam*' at the head of our exercises in Euclid and '*Quod erat demonstrandum*' at the end, and wished that the fate of Burke and Hare had befallen Hall and Knight and Hall and Stephens.

Teachers who had previously taught me mathematics

were heard to say that they thought it entirely true that not even Rowan Hamilton or Einstein could ever get me to pass Matriculation in that subject, but Brother Evangelist did it. It cannot have been easy. Only the ball-frame could be of any help to someone like myself to whom figures have always been, and continue to be, meaningless and who has never been able to see why any two sides of a triangle are together greater than the third. Brother Evangelist did, it is true, invoke the aid of Higher Powers when on the day before the maths examination he said to me, 'There's nothing now for it but prayer and the sacraments.' Examination day remains in my memory chiefly for the ripple of laughter that ran around the hall when the superintendent handed me logarithm tables. They might as well have been the Dead Sea Scrolls.

For English we had Tim O'Donoghue and, later, Sean Connolly. Each in his own way was an inspired teacher. O'Donoghue's method was to talk discursively of literature and life in such a stimulating way that he had us all borrowing Chekhov and Turgenev from the Public Library, which was then in Tuckey Street. He paid little attention to the syllabus, scorned inspectors and derided the learning of poetry by rote. I often met him after I had left university and become a teacher, when he was to be found during hot July days sitting comfortably in Tony Moynihan's bar at the top of Wyse's Hill examining Leaving Certificate scripts. He did so at a table in the snug of which were large rings left by pint glasses and, as he ripped open the large envelopes, he would mutter, 'Just like gutting herrings.'

Connolly's gift as a teacher lay in the way he awakened in us an awareness of, and a feeling for, the beauty of words. He deplored any reference to 'the examination course', which he considered a denigrating phrase. Instead of attempting to forecast questions, he gave us an understanding of how to experience a poem, to savour the sound as well as the sense, the colour as well as the content. His concern was beauty and how the poet's imaginative use of words reveals that beauty.

History I came to study only when my science career was terminated by Mr O'Reilly because of certain liberties I had taken in the mixing of acids. It was a change which brought an unexpected financial return. Our history teacher, Mr Harty, suggested that as we were studying the War of the Spanish Succession during which the battle of Blenheim was fought, and as the examination was taking place on the day of the Derby in which a horse with the name Blenheim was engaged, a visit to the bookmaker might not be inappropriate. Blenheim won. I can recall the year, 1930, the starting-price, 18 to 1, and the jockey's name, Harry Wragg. The nearby shops, Campbells and Macari's on Washington Street, did good business in ice-cream and lemonade that summer's day.

Most schools invariably endeavour to impress prospective parents by singing the praises of their most illustrious Old Boys. 'Pres', as one might expect in a city where superlatives are common currency, was no exception. There were photographs, mostly framed sepia ones, in all the classrooms of ex-students who had served in the Indian Civil Service. What I wonder did the native princes make of the Cork accent which, if one believes the photos, must have echoed through the provinces where these satraps and proconsuls, moustached and cane-carrying, administered British rule? By presenting their pictures for our daily admiration, did the superior, Brother Connolly, hope to ensure that the sun would never set on the Empire while Corkmen were at its service! They were still in its service as late as 1918 when an advertisement in *The Cork Examiner* stated that pupils were prepared for the army entrances to Sandhurst, Wellington and Quetta Royal Military Colleges.

As the glories of Empire receded, it was to the professions and the banks that school-leavers in Pres and elsewhere turned their attention. The old Munster Bank had accepted boys on the nomination of the school superior, and when bank examinations were introduced Presentation College formed a special bank class. For many years the Munster and Leinster Bank was largely staffed by ex-pupils of Cork schools.* Small wonder then that Corkmen everywhere sing with such enthusiasm of 'the banks of my own lovely Lee'!

Cork people, or so it seems to me, have at all times been inordinately proud of their origins. We never questioned the superiority of our school, of our teachers, of our teams. Thus, it was no more than we expected when in 1926-27 the Pres hurling team won the Munster Senior Schools Cup and went on to win the Munster Senior Schools Cup in rugby. The hurlers had no ambition to become rugby players but when their arch-rivals, Christian College, objected (unsuccessfully) to the hurling team, it was decided that they would have to be taught a lesson. My memory is of Tim O'Driscoll, the captain, later to become director-general of Bord Fáilte, bringing the cups around to the various

*In the summer of 1931, when I left school, *The Cork Examiner* published the results of the Matriculation Examination: 41 pupils of Presentation College were successful; 23 entered university and 9 (including 6 who had taken the separate Munster and Leinster Bank examination) entered the bank.

classrooms. In the years that followed, that most evil statute, Rule 31 of the Gaelic Athletic Association, was invoked to ensure that never again did Pres boys welcome a victorious captain in both hurling and rugby.

The divisions among boys of the school-going population spilled over to the girls. Pres boys were supposed to be favoured by those attending St Aloysius or St Maries of the Isle, while the girls of St Angela's on Patrick's Hill were attracted towards 'Christians'. Divisions were temporarily forgotten on Sunday evenings when those who possessed invitations gathered for decorous and well-supervised dancing at the Oratory on St Mary's Road.

Whatever superiority the products of Presentation College and Christian College believed they enjoyed in the social life of the city was not mirrored in the world of academic achievement. There the more practical approach of the Christian Brothers was typified by the North Monastery and Sullivan's Quay, and sixty years have done nothing to alter my conviction that the most thorough preparation for examinations is that given in their schools.

The Bishop of Cork, like his episcopal colleagues in other parts of Ireland, saw to it that the diocesan seminary, Farranferris, did not have to face competition from the religious teaching orders. Education was not considered a suitable field for the exercise of Christian charity. Dr Daniel Coholan, when Bishop of Cork, is said to have turned down a suggestion that the Jesuits might be permitted to open a college in the city. Breandán Ó hEithir in *Over the Bar* quoted the reply attributed to the bishop when someone pointed out that it was strange that the Jesuit Order had never established a school in Cork: 'I would regard that as a remarkable manifestation of the power of prayer.'

Outside the walls of the schoolroom, most Cork people who achieved material success tended to move upwards and outwards, first to Sunday's Well and Montenotte, and later to Douglas and Blackrock. As late as the early 'thirties leading business men still came into their offices by bus and I can remember seeing them taking down the shutters on shopfronts as I hurried through the streets eager to get to school before 9 o'clock and 'cog' some homework left undone. The city was then so small and compact that almost all office workers, bank clerks and those employed in the big drapery shops such as The Queen's Old Castle, Dwyers, Cashs and Grants, returned home for dinner at 1 o'clock. A certain formality of dress was expected of most clerks and the 'walkers' in drapery shops invariably wore dark jackets, striped trousers and white shirts with stiff collars.

Social divisions, often blurred on working days, were sharply in evidence on Sundays. The churches of St Mary's (known as 'the Sand Quay Church' to an older generation) and of SS. Peter and Paul would have received 'U' certification from Nancy Mitford, as would the Wesleyan church in Patrick Street, St Finbarr's Cathedral and the Presbyterian church at the foot of Summerhill. Attendance at Sunday worship in these churches may not have had quite the social cachet of being seen in the Royal enclosure at Ascot, but it ran it close.

* * *

Having matriculated in 1931, I went in the autumn of that year to University College, Cork, paid my year's fee of £12.2s.0d. to Mr Joseph Downey, secretary and bursar, and became a student in the Faculty of Arts. It was then a small university of some 500 students. We knew all the professors, saw them cutting their lawns, walking their dogs and cycling to lectures. We knew their hobbies, their interests and often their political views.

The older ones knew what was expected of them; they wore tattered gowns, had long beards and were absent-minded. In this respect Professor Stockley, who had the distinction of being appointed Professor of English to the Queen's College in 1905 and re-appointed to University College, Cork, in 1909, fulfilled expectations. In addition, he was a superb lecturer. His prose was splendid if highly convoluted and, as was said of another such writer, few readers had the staying power to make the long trip from one of his full stops to the next. The story is told that his successor in the Chair of English, Daniel Corkery, on meeting him one day, expressed the hope that he, Stockley, would die before him. On being asked why, he is said to have replied, 'I don't want anyone to write about me in such imperishable but impenetrable prose.'

Alfred O'Rahilly, Professor of Maths Physics, was also prepared, metaphorically speaking, to get up on a tub and harangue the citizens. I once heard him speaking from the steps leading to *The Cork Examiner* opposite the old Victoria Hotel. The words tumbled out at a speed few speakers ever equalled; indeed few can ever have compressed so many words into a short speech and fewer still aroused so much antagonism among a crowd to whom, at that time, purely social issues did not seem to mean much. A much more quiet and unassuming man, Professor James Hogan, spoke persuasively and eloquently on Cumann na nGael platforms, but he was more suited to the lecture theatre than to the tumult of street corners.

Among the professors whose lectures I attended, Isaac Swain, Professor of Geology and Geography, was outstanding. He had come from County Antrim and in the best tradition of Quakers his house, 'Slemish', on the Glasheen Road and his bungalow near Weaver's Point, Crosshaven, were ever open to students. Tall and distinguished in appearance, he shared with Professor Sperrin-Johnson the biology block, a semi-autonomous fief near the Honan Chapel. Engineers as well as teachers benefited from the tours he organized to ensure that the physical and geological features of the country would not remain 'dead' in the pages of a textbook.

A succession of fine writers – Dowden, Stockley and Corkery – had made the Department of English Literature in the university particularly strong and, at a time when the Cork University Press was very active, it is regrettable that almost nothing of the work of their students was ever published. Five graduate students, all known to me, were at one time writing M.A. theses on Carolan, Gerald Griffin, James Fintan Lalor, Canon Sheehan and the Banim brothers. These theses now rest in their expensive bindings gathering dust in 'the Maltings'.

Corkery believed that *Synge and Anglo-Irish Literature*, published in 1931, was the work for which he would be remembered. He was inclined to dismiss *The Hidden Ireland* (1925), regretting that he had not written it in Irish! Oddly enough, he was always willing to discuss English Literature with his students in Irish. He certainly did so with me on the many occasions that I cycled out to his home near Kilumney to have tea with himself and his sister. His Irish made me think of the early enthusiasts for the language who had learned it from O'Growney's texts. It was stiff and at times almost laboured as he sought to find the word or phrase to express his thoughts.

Corkery was endlessly patient and endlessly helpful to those who sought his advice, and his own work influenced the writing of many of the younger generation. He taught them the necessity of discipline and prepared them to set down in the barest prose the significant episodes that reveal human destiny. All his thoughts were honestly held, all he wrote was sincerely written, and to the end he remained true to his belief that 'No work of any significance will ever again come out of Ireland until we end the colonial tradition. The choice for us is between Irish and Provincialism.'

It was unfortunate that at a time when the English department was prospering, the Irish faculty[1] should have been less vigorous, less enterprising. While Professor 'Torna' O Donnchadha was a scholar of distinction, neither his brother Éamon nor Cormac Ó Cuilleanáin – both lecturers – seemed to inspire much enthusiasm among their students. *An Chuallacht*, the Irish society in the college, languished and not until the *Comhcaidreamh* was launched in the early 'forties did the language movement again gather momentum. While it is unfair to select one work as an example of what was being done in the post-graduate field of Irish studies, it nevertheless points to a certain sterility. 'The use of the preposition in the works of An t-Athair Peadar Ó Laoghaire' was the singularly restrictive title of a thesis embarked on by a Kerry student of my year.

At a time when the Irish language was distancing itself from the methods which had long served the Gaelic League, the Professor of Anatomy, Dr MacConaill, was insisting on the use of Irish where possible in his department. He compiled a vocabulary of terms and with all the zeal of the convert (he had learned the language while a prisoner on the *Argenta* in Belfast Lough during the war), he sought to encourage his students to use them.

Looking back on those university days my memory is of a carefree time with few of the pressures to which students are now subject. We 'cut' lectures with impunity and when we did attend whiled away the time filling in football coupons and selecting cross-doubles. There was then no limit to the number of years spent taking a degree and so there were always a number of 'ancients' to be found in the billiards-room or discussing such matters as the relative merits of 'The Western Star' and 'The Courthouse Tavern', two public-houses within walking distance of the college. We sold lockers, seats in lecture halls and membership of non-existent college societies to 'jibs', first-year students who were easily recognizable as they wandered around the quadrangle.

By present-day standards we were undoubtedly immature. It may have been the Matriculation examination, almost always taken in Fifth Year, introduced many to university life at too young an age. Or, and this was equally true of countries other than Ireland, youth and adolescence saw life as something to be enjoyed and savoured. It was after all the 'thirties, and there were few clouds that did not break to let the sunshine through.

TWO

Good Counsel College

> Ireland had a great tradition of revolution, yet the revolution changed nothing. When the English moved out the Church stepped in.
>
> Sean Kenny, *A Paler Shade of Green*

WHEN IN 1936 I began to study the market for Arts graduates, I found that while there were no barriers to lay men and women entering the teaching profession, it was nevertheless largely in the hands of religious. The education they offered was selective both in the location of their schools and in the procedures they adopted for admitting pupils to these schools. They were greatly encouraged by the favour shown them by successive native governments terrified of being accused of anti-Catholic bias and by the Catholic hierarchy who, by their open hostility to the founding of schools by lay teachers, deliberately reduced the latter to a subordinate role.

The obduracy of the hierarchy and the autocratic manner in which it controlled the extension of post-primary schooling was referred to by Garret FitzGerald during a Senate debate on education, in the course of which he said:

> We all know that in this country there has been a conflict, for a century or more, between the hierarchy and the religious orders. Let us get this thing straight and talk straight about it now. The conflict has meant that in many dioceses religious orders have not been allowed to open schools – so that the monopoly of the diocesan college has been maintained – which, in turn, means totally inadequate provision for secondary education . . . The bishops have, in this respect, I believe put their own private interests before the interests of the country at large, as any group of people are likely to do on some occasions.*

I have always resented what I consider to be the intrusion of religious, of all denominations, in education. Religious education, by all means, for those who want it, but education in the control of religious for the purpose of conveying a religious message, I would oppose. I have seen how shallow is the pretext that religion matters when, as examination time drew near, religious education threatened to get in the way of secular subjects. It was never allowed to do so. It was dropped from the time-table. Good examination results meant more pupils and more pupils meant more money, so spiritual values were sacrificed on the altar of material gain.

Having unburdened myself of those personal prejudices, I must admit that I was very grateful when an Augustinian priest, Father Colman O'Driscoll of Courtmacsherry, offered me my first teaching post in Good Counsel College, New Ross, one of the two boarding

---

**Seanad Éireann*, 9 February 1967.

colleges owned by the order in Ireland. I was appointed as a teacher of General Subjects. That ambiguous-sounding title was understood by teachers to mean that you did everything except latrine duty.

The college had a long and rather uneven history. In the years after the passing of the Act of Catholic Emancipation the number of pupils rose by ninety, then fell so low that the school was closed down and re-opened only in 1890. When Edward Ensor, inspector of the Intermediate Education Board, arrived there on 26 January 1910 there were but thirty-six boys in residence.

The staff at that time consisted of Mr de Lacy and one regular assistant, an untrained teacher named Harmon. All classes were held in one room and in describing the general appearance of the school, Mr Ensor used the opaque phrase 'as clean as possible in the circumstances'. For a school which in later years was to earn an enviable reputation for high standards of work and scholarship, the report of the inspector was far from flattering: 'All the classes in this school are in a state of chaos, owing to the absence, from illness, of Father Doyle, who has been away since November. His substitute, an aged priest, knows little or nothing about Latin.'

The physical well-being of the boys was, however, well seen to and under the heading 'Recreation', Ensor listed drill with 'marching, wands, dumb-bells, Indian clubs and parallel bars'. The ventilation was commented upon as being 'by means of windows', as if they were an invention of recent date. These were presumably the ancestors of the windows which in my time were formally closed in October of each year and opened in May of the year following. It needed only someone like Black Rod to invest the opening with a certain ceremony.

My room in what was referred to as the new block was little more than a spirit-depressing square, twelve feet by nine, bleak enough to seduce a hermit. The one window looked out on sagging rooftops and dismal backyards. A prie-dieu, a table, a chair, an oleograph of the Pope, a two-bar electric fire and an iron bedstead were evidently considered ample furnishings for someone whose unending work would make him indifferent to his surroundings. There are some who believe that such frugal comfort leads to high thinking. They are mistaken. It does not.

The dormitory was furnished with regulation iron bedsteads, and icy draughts direct from the Steppes came up the river every winter to freeze the occupants. When the water froze in the holy-water font at the door, a dispensation (confined to the diocese of Ferns) was given to anyone not making the sign of the cross as he went out.

I may have been wrong to expect more luxurious surroundings since the pension at the time was a modest £45 a year. For that sum, the boys were housed and fed and taught. They were almost all on scholarship from national schools and came from every county in Ireland. The accommodation was adequate, the tuition excellent but the food would have justified Mark Twain's observation that 'We didn't starve but nobody ate chicken unless we were sick or the chicken was.' One of the tenets of catering in boarding-schools is that boys need nutrition only at stated and well-separated intervals. This is so clearly false that it scarcely needs contradiction. Sister Bernard's pantry was raided periodically by ravenous boarders who, possibly because the raids took place at night, failed to read the notice which said 'The kitchen and pantry are out of bounds.'

As a teacher of General Subjects in an 'A' school,* I taught Latin, History and Geography through Irish as well as English, and Irish to the Matriculation class. (If a teacher were given such a work-load today, a teachers' union would have a picket on the school before first class ended.) I took Games every fifth day which, in turn, was considered to be a 'Duty day' for each of the five lay teachers on the staff. On a Duty day I was with the boys from 6.45 a.m. when I went through the dormitories ringing a bell and chanting 'Laudator Jesus Christus' until at 10 p.m. I rang another bell to mark the end of Study and the end of another school day. John Betjeman could well have had that boarding school in mind when he wrote,

> The schoolboy sense of impending doom
> Which goes with news of death and clanging bells . . .
> Doom! Shivering doom! Inexorable bells
> To early school, to chapel, school again:
> Compulsory constipation, hurried meals . . .
> The dread of beatings! Dread of being late!

I do not know if you have ever been, for the best part of fifteen hours, in charge of the emotional, intellectual, spiritual and nutritional life of one hundred boys ageing from twelve to eighteen. If you have not, then add a supplement to your prayers that you never will be. History does not record that Henry VIII attended a religious-controlled boarding school but had he done so there would at least be

*In 1935-36 when I began teaching there were seventy-seven 'A' schools in the Republic. In 1983-84 there were fourteen such schools. By definition, an 'A' school was one in which all subjects other than English were taught through the medium of Irish.

a ready explanation for his eagerness to dissolve all monasteries.

What enabled the teachers to hold on to their sanity was the certainty that severe punishment awaited anyone who broke the rules. A boy who came to Good Counsel College thinking that the cane was an anachronistic relic of an earlier age had second thoughts after visiting the Dean of Discipline. The latter observed the biblical injunction that 'whatsoever thy hand findeth to do, do it with all thy might'. And, as he was a man of fifteen stone weight, what his hand found to do was done with impressive vigour.

The rich variety of subjects that I was asked to teach was normal enough in secondary schools at the time. The Department of Education was too frightened of the religious to insist on teachers taking only those subjects on their degree, and the day of the specialist teacher was still far away. In fact the Department rarely questioned whether the teachers had degrees. In that respect 1937 was little different from 1917 when Bertram Windle, later to become President of University College, Cork, applied for a certificate to teach in Ireland. On the strength of his Bachelor of Arts degree he was given a certificate to teach and earn grants in all the forty-eight subjects, including Naval Architecture, listed under the South Kensington Examination Board!

My teaching was mostly done in a basement cloakroom which should surely have laid the Augustinian fathers open to prosecution under some kind of academic Factory Act. Oddly enough there was a fireplace in that cloakroom, but as the chimney seemed permanently choked it served only to deepen the existing gloom. That was in 1936 when par. 3 of the General Regulations for Continued Recognition of Secondary Schools read, 'The school premises must be suitable as regards accommodation, equipment, lighting, heating, and sanitation.' Even a skilled sophist might have found it difficult to reconcile my basement environment with the Augustinian interpretation of that paragraph.

A pupil in the back row could have died without any notice being taken unless, of course, an inspector happened to arrive. On such occasions, the back row which accommodated all 'the lower stream pupils' was sent off to hide wherever they pleased until the 'All Clear' was sounded. Generally, they took refuge in the confessional boxes of the College chapel, there to read any pornographic literature available.

Of the inspectors on the Eastern circuit, the most feared was undoubtedly Tadhg Ó Tuama. He belonged to the 'hog, dog, or devil'* school of Irish enthusiasts to whom the revival of the language took precedence over purely educational aims. Ó Tuama did not always content himself with observing the teacher's performance, preferring when possible to give a demonstration lesson himself. He put on a most impressive show during one of my classes where, to illustrate the use of the different tenses of the verb *ith*, 'to eat', he ate his way through a pupil's sandwiches!

In those days an inspector usually spent two to three days in a town where there was more than one secondary school. Some, like John Bithrey who had been appointed as

---

*Seoirse MacNiocaill, Chief Inspector of the Department of Education, to whom the remark is attributed, was a man of great energy and determination. At a meeting in Kilkenny held by the Gaelic League, of which he was a member of the *Coisde Gnótha*, he made the stirring pronouncement that 'they were going to make Irish the language of the country, and he did not care what hog, dog, or devil stood in the way they were going to smite them' (quoted in *The Leader*, Vol. LII, No. 5, 6 March 1926).

far back as 1910 and who inspected a class of mine in Kilkenny as late as 1941, moved from room to room with all the gravity of a surgeon doing the round of hospital wards. When he indicated his intention of remaining to observe a lesson, he carefully arranged a hand-knit rug over his shoulders, assured himself that his chair was not in a draught and, if it was winter, asked what the room temperature was. He lived to be ninety-two.

Inspectors were much in evidence in those years; they were the eyes and ears of a Department as yet unsure of itself. They prowled and probed, recommended texts, not infrequently those which they had written, unerringly selected the dullest pupil to question and departed with the blessings, in Irish if it was an 'A' school, of principal and staff. Today, the inspector is a quasi-extinct occupational species.

For all the power inspectors exercised over teachers and the curriculum, they seemed powerless to effect any improvement in the physical conditions within the school. In my lifetime I have known pupils to come with sods of turf for the classroom fire and I have worn in class not a gown and mortar-board but a warm overcoat, scarf and gloves. This would most likely have met with the approval of Dom Sweetman, who was headmaster of Mount St Benedict in the 'twenties. One of his rules was that pupils were allowed to wear an overcoat in school but not outside!

There were very few day boys at Good Counsel College in the 'thirties probably because of the existence of another secondary school run by the Christian Brothers in the town, and I do not think that any effort was made to attract them. For Protestants there was the John Ivory School dating back to 1713. The headmaster, Mr Bush, had but one assistant, William le Blanc, and after his departure and when the numbers on the roll had dropped to single figures, the school closed in 1945.

The great good fortune that Good Counsel College enjoyed lay in its staff. Its academic reputation rested firmly on four teachers, each of whom came there from university and remained until retirement. Toby Kavanagh, who took Irish, had not far to come as his people farmed at The Rower in County Kilkenny. Maurice Foley, when a schoolboy at St Brendan's, Killarney, had led Ireland in Latin and Greek at the certificate examinations, and these he taught to successive generations in New Ross. Jack Moore, champion long jumper in his youth, taught Mathematics thus maintaining the tradition of scholarship in that discipline long associated with his own school, St Michael's, Listowel. Noel O'Mahony, who had once thought of making his career as a violinist, chose instead to teach English which he had studied in his native Cork under Professor Stockley.

Four men whose span of teaching service in the one school totalled almost two hundred years!

Sporting activities in New Ross, as in most provincial towns at the time, were largely confined to Gaelic games. Unlike other parts of Wexford, New Ross had a strong hurling tradition and the O'Hanrahan Club was always represented on the county team. The other local club, the Geraldines, inclined more to Gaelic football and their ground at Barrett's Park* was loaned to the College for practice purposes. The College won the Leinster Colleges Junior Hurling Cup in 1936 though, oddly enough, no

*The two clubs have since amalgamated and Barrett's Park is now called the O'Kennedy Park in honour of Sean O'Kennedy, captain of the great Wexford hurling and football teams of the 1914-18 period.

shield on the plinth commemorates that victory.

The town was a depressed area in the 'thirties. Cherry's Brewery, the Cable Factory and the newly established Steele and Company were almost the only employers of labour within the town. During my stay in New Ross I often walked the boys in crocodile formation to the Pink Rocks on the Waterford Road without ever seeing a ship anchor in that splendid estuary. 'Cot' fishermen there were in plenty and also numerous steam barges going up river to St Mullins or down to Waterford. I saw one of the cots or coracles in the making, out of willow and hazel, with calico covered in pitch over the frame.

Memories of 1798 were revived during my last year in the town when the 140th anniversary of the '98 Rebellion was celebrated with all the defiant pageantry with which the Irish commemorate military defeats. 'Boolavogue' was sung in countless bars and in a variety of voices, bands paraded to the familiar sounds of 'Kelly the Boy from Killane' and saucers of milk appeared on doorsteps on the way up to the Bullaun to show that the treachery of 'the cats' from a neighbouring county had not been forgotten. I can still recall one stanza of a fine recording of 'Boolavogue' written for Feis Carman by Donnchadh Ó Laoghaire, then living in Wexford town:

I mBuaile Mhaodóg tráthnóna gréine,
Is bánta Lughra go geal faoi bhláth;
Bhí teinte-cnámha ar bhárr na sléibhte
Do bhailig céadta chun dul san ár.
Ó Chill gheal Chormaic, bhí an tAthair Seán ann,
Is a sluaite lámh leis chun dul sa ghleo:
Is mhóidig feasta gurabh é ár dtaoiseach
A treorú Gaedhil an fhaid bheadh beo.

My leaving the employment of the Order of St Augustine, Bishop of Hippo, was more abrupt than I would have wished. The certificate examinations began as was customary in the first week of June and the headmaster, Father Conlan, came to me on the Monday of that week to inform me that he thought that by agreement we should part. That meant that I was dismissed and there was nothing I could do but agree with him. Few religious orders provided their staff with contracts of employment, and few lay teachers were prepared to accuse them of unfair dismissal.

One effect of those years in an all-Irish school was to chill my enthusiasm for the language. It did not kill it but it did convince me that the inspectors who so earnestly advocated the teaching of subjects through Irish were mistaken. In the absence of an accepted terminology, in the absence of any textbooks of quality, in the absence even of teachers with the required knowledge and fluency, why were they so insistent? Breathnach, Ó Siochfhradha, MacNiocaill, Ó Tuama, Ó Raifeartaigh were all men of high academic attainments, well aware that no effort had been made to prepare the ground for the revival of a language for long discouraged, for long unused.

They pushed aside all educational arguments against making use of the schools for that purpose. That they did damage is certain and while the degree of damage is not easily quantified, it made for an imbalance that took many years to rectify. The Sciences and Modern Languages suffered most simply because there were no textbooks in Irish for the teaching of these subjects. Some perfectly appalling textbooks were available to the teacher of History and Geography which, were they extensively used, would have reduced the teaching of those subjects in the higher classes to the level of the Sixth Standard in a national school. They saw nothing ludicrous in a pupil getting marks *in excess of the maximum* by answering any paper other than Art and English through Irish. They pushed ahead with a zeal worthy, as the cliché has it, of a better cause.

The most objectionable aspect of the revival programme was the deliberate injection of money in the 'A' schools where often the teaching through Irish was no more than a façade. The Irish equivalents for certain vital words and phrases in Maths and Science were learnt, discarded for most of the year, only to be quickly recalled before examination day. Public money went to the schools which took part in the deception, public money went to the teachers who connived at it, public money went to the authors and publishers of texts who profited by it.

Why did it continue for so long? One explanation is the need of the schools for money. It must be remembered that there was no money for the building of secondary schools, very little for maintenance and even less for heating. Why did not school authorities and more especially school principals protest against the distortion of true education? There is one explanation and it may be as good as any. The religious authorities who owned almost all second-level schools were interested in the control of education and to a much lesser degree in the content. Bearing this in mind, it is not without significance that Christian Doctrine was excluded from the policy of compulsion because, according to Miss Laura Gavan Duffy writing in *The Leader*, it was such an important subject and that technical terms might be difficult. I feel that she might simply have said that the Catholic Church would not permit it.

Nor was the public attitude unaffected by what was

accepted as State policy. From being looked upon by some as part of our heritage to be valued and preserved, and by others as an unnecessary encumbrance for their children, it came to be considered by many as a mere vehicle for self-advancement. The schools that earned extra money committing themselves to the teaching of subjects through Irish were not demonstrably better than other schools, the teachers who earned more money were not necessarily more competent, nor were the pupils more advanced. Writing at a time when the tide against compulsion was beginning to turn, the Professor of Irish in University College, Cork, had this to say:

> There is no doubt that the continuous use of pressure methods to propagate Irish in the schools has killed much of the love, joy and pride proper to the teaching and learning of the language; in the absence of these, the study, its patriotic motive obscured or lost, ceases to have any real meaning and bears only Dead Sea Fruit.*

The overall result was that 'compulsory Irish' became a pantomime joke, a source of facetious comment, an excuse to clothe incompetence and, not infrequently, a cause of bitter resentment.

The language remains a subject on which the last word is ever unlikely to be said. Any experience I have leads me to believe that young people are increasingly aware of the richness and beauty of their linguistic inheritance and, given the present enthusiasm for Irish songs and Irish music, the subject will gain rather than lose once it ceases to be compul-

---

*Professor R. A. Breathnach, *Studies*, Summer 1956.

sory. The obligatory oral tests in the civil service and also for some diplomas in the universities are regarded with cynicism, nor can it be otherwise given the nature of such measurements of linguistic competence.

THREE

St Fachtna's — Lota House

THE SCHOOL IN SKIBBEREEN, County Cork, to which I came in the autumn of 1938 was dedicated to St Fachtna and run by the De La Salle Brothers. It had absorbed the much older 'University and Intermediate School' which was founded in 1878 with Mr Edward Hogan as principal. Schools with such titles, usually with lay principals, would appear to have succeeded the 'hedge schools', and they lived a precarious existence until the written examination came to replace patronage as a means of entry whether to the British army, navy or civil service. Then, when it seemed that they might have prospered and given the lay teacher an alternative to the emigrant ship, there came the wave of religious-inspired enthusiasm for teaching and the lay teacher was relegated to a subordinate if not a menial position.

If we are to judge from an advertisement published in *The Eagle and County Cork Advertiser* of 1 July 1882, Edward Hogan's school was a lay school only in name. The advertisement ran as follows:

> This School is Established under the Patronage of the Most Rev. the Bishop and Clergy of the Diocese, and

supplies a high-class literary and professional education. Preparation for the Universities, Ecclesiastical Colleges, Sciences and Art, and Intermediate Examinations. Business resumed on Monday, 24th July, on which day all Pupils are required to return punctually, as classes for all the above Examinations will be formed at once. Terms and Honours List on application to the Principal.

Principal: Mr E. L. Hogan, C.U.
Assistant: Mr Daniel McCarthy.

In that same year Patrick Harrington and John J. Sheehy passed in Senior Grade, and Edmund Cotter, John Harrington, Daniel Collins, Daniel Donovan, Timothy O'Donovan and Francis J. Ward passed in Junior Grade.

The story of the coming of the Brothers to Skibbereen had its background in a controversy which had gone on for almost eighty years in another part of Ireland. On 6 December 1859 Mrs Julia Conmee, a well-to-do Catholic living in Roscommon, made her will. Under the terms of this will she requested that when all other legacies had been paid, the residue of her property should be handed over to the superior-general of the Institute of the Brothers of the Christian Schools in Ireland and his two assistants-general, as trustees for the establishment of a school for the education of poor male children.

The Christian Brothers were, it appears, quite willing to do so, but the provision, maintenance and staffing of such a school was at the time beyond their means. Letters passed between the bishop of the diocese (Elphin) and successive superior-generals of the Christian Brothers. From these it is clear that the real obstacle was the effect that another second-level school would be likely to have on the numbers in the diocesan seminary. The bishop chose to ignore the many resolutions passed by public bodies asking that the Christian Brothers be introduced into the town.

That nothing was done for seventy years to make use of Mrs Conmee's bequest has to be attributed to episcopalian intransigence. In what he must have hoped would break the deadlock, the bishop had the parish priest of Roscommon town, Father Cummins, write to the superior-general of the Christian Brothers informing him that 'the Bishop, as far as I know his mind, is willing to receive you provided you undertake no Secondary teaching, but devote yourself to the programme of Technical Schools, or that of an Agricultural College.'* These conditions, not unexpectedly, the Christian Brothers found unacceptable.

In the summer of 1930 Brother Shanahan of the De La Salle order went, on the invitation of the bishop, to Roscommon as principal of the national school, the headmaster of which had retired. Some of the townspeople, fearing that this might mean the end of their hopes of having the Christian Brothers, called a meeting to protest against what they considered to be a contravention of Mrs Conmee's intentions. The bishop saw this as a defiance of his authority and in a letter, read at all the Masses on the Sunday morning of the meeting, said, 'We are pained that a public meeting has been summoned with a view to discussing the school question which we, the Bishop of the Diocese, have already decided.'**

On the day of the public meeting, Monsignor Cummins, addressing the congregation at all the Masses,

---

*2 September 1920.

**17 August 1930.

stated that he objected to being summoned to a meeting from the dead walls of the town and, in a reference to those responsible for calling the meeting, said:

> It was the act not of the old stock of Roscommon but of the ignorant rabble of the town, some of whom were only a few years in the parish and got very little respect in the place they came from. If these Brothers [the Irish Christian Brothers] came into the parish they would probably starve and beggar the schools . . . . No matter what meetings are held, the Irish Christian Brothers would never come into the parish.

The bishop made use of almost identical words in the course of a letter to the provincial, Brother Brendan O'Herlihy, of the De La Salle order. His letter in which he rejected a proposal to have the De La Salle Brothers in the primary school and the Christian Brothers in the secondary, ended with the words 'but we will never agree to allow the Christian Brothers into Roscommon in any capacity'.

In an effort to have the matter decided once and for all, a Schools Committee which had been set up in the town decided to seek legal advice. The case of the Conmee Bequest came before Judge Johnston in the High Court in July 1931. The court asked that as a first step all monies in the hands of the trustees should be lodged in court. A scheme was then prepared for the use of these monies and a defence was entered by the ecclesiastical authorities. Before a date for the hearing was fixed, the Catholic hierarchy, fearing unwelcome publicity, sent word through the Papal Nuncio that the parties concerned should withdraw the case from the civil courts and submit the issue to Rome. This was done and on 23 July 1936 the judges gave their verdict. In substance it said that the right of administering the legacy of Mrs Conmee belonged to the Irish Christian Brothers.

While the litigation was making its tedious way through the courts, the De La Salle order had actually opened a secondary school in Roscommon. When the decision of the Roman Curia was announced, the Bishop of Elphin was obliged to write to the provincial asking that his Brothers be withdrawn from the school. Within a month of their departure, they were installed in a temporary residence in North Street, Skibbereen. The first intimation the townspeople had of their coming was when the Bishop of Ross, Dr Casey, speaking at 12 o'clock Mass on the first Sunday in August, announced that he had invited them to take over the school where Mr Duggan had for long laboured alone.

I came to know Daniel Duggan well and can remember him telling me that he had been taught Latin, Greek and a little French by 'a spoiled priest' named Cadogan who lived near Skehanoir on the road to Ballydehob. His school seems to have led a precarious existence and when Edward Ensor of the Board of Intermediate Education arrived there on inspection in 1909, there were but twenty pupils. Duggan, whose modest qualifications for school-mastering showed him to have been a 2nd Arts student in the Royal University and a candidate for the B.A. degree, had taken over the school from Hogan in 1900. At that time he had no assistant and taught all subjects in one 'badly lighted' room. Ensor's report revealed the lack of what today would be considered certain essential amenities. Under the heading 'Description of Schoolhouse', we find 'Urinals: None; Lavatories: None.' Nor was any provision made for activities outside of the classroom. Under the heading 'Recreation', Ensor noted 'Games organized by staff: None; Compulsory Games: None; Drill: None; Provision of exercise for all: None; Provision of exercise on wet days: None.'

The academic standing of the school seems to have been in keeping with the unpretentious nature of the building. Of the two pupils taking Junior Grade French, one was said by the inspector to be a persistent truant who 'does not attend more than once a week and knows nothing'. Nor did the headmaster escape criticism. Ensor observed that 'his articulation is extremely indistinct . . . and it is hard to follow and understand him'.

Poor Mr Duggan! It cannot have been easy to teach school, with never more than one other to share the burden, for almost forty years and live on the fees, rarely more than a few shillings a term, and the meagre Results Fees payable on the handful of examination candidates. He enjoyed the company of the other headmasters living in the town and Austen Sweetman, principal of Abbeystrewery School, and Jer MacCarthy, principal of the Abbey School, were amongt his closest friends. He had a fine library of classical literature and treasured in particular a copy of *The Council Book of the Corporation of Youghal 1610-1800*.

My own arrival in the town coincided with Glandore Regatta and my landlady, Tess O'Brien of Bridge Street, suggested that I should cycle over to it. She gave me directions to 'go east the road past Shepperton Lakes until you come to Leap and then follow the signpost'. When I reached Glandore I looked down on a scene of enchantment: a landlocked harbour where dozens of pleasure boats, some four-oared racing boats and a few small yachts swayed at anchor against the background of cream-washed houses and wooded hills.

Glandore Regatta is not, as you may think, an occasion when sun-bright parasols shade summer frocks and striped blazers while swift outriggers skim over the water with blades flashing in the sun. Rather it is an occasion when the oarsmen, for the most part seated happily on upturned barrels, seem unwilling to put to sea, when oars are with difficulty fitted into rowlocks and, when they do, the oars rarely rise and fall in unison. Nobody minds very much if the evening shadows have begun to lengthen by the time the loudspeaker asks crews for the first race to go to the starting-point. It's a day out and the night is far advanced before the sounds of 'Skibbereen' and 'Bantry Bay' die away over the water.

The day at Glandore Regatta was an almost ideal introduction to life in one of the most pleasant towns in Ireland. A little over a week later came Ballydehob Sports, held in a field overlooking 'Carbery's Hundred Isles'. I travelled there in a manner which may have been unique in railway history. An excursion train, with an open observation car at the rear, left Skibbereen at mid-day. It was no more than a mile outside the town when it stopped and began to reverse. This caused the paggengers to look at one another 'in a wild surmise' and question such odd behaviour on the part of the train. The answer was to be seen in a Pickwickian figure on the platform. 'Sonny' Goggin, director of the Skibbereen-Schull Tramway and Light Railway Company, had been forgotten!

The sports meeting brought together all the notable athletes of County Cork and beyond. And there, to add to the glory of the autumn day, was Danno Mahony, champion wrestler of the world. His brother, Florrie, was a competitor and at the end of the day when neither he nor Maurice Curtin, the Irish champion, succeeded in throwing the 56 lb shot over the bar at 16 feet, Danno was invited to have a throw. I can recall the moment when he stood up, loosened the collar of his shirt and, after an upward glance, threw the weight high over the bar with inches to spare. It was a perfect ending to a day that had in it echoes of *Knocknagow* and the feats of Mat the Thresher.

My return to Skibbereen that evening, like my departure in the morning, was not without incident. I was invited for a drink at a hotel which was situated convenient to the railway station. During the evening a loud knock, followed by the announcement 'Guards on duty', sent the customers scurrying to seek refuge as glasses were hurriedly emptied and lights turned off. One customer simply went into a bedroom where he was later found with his bowler hat and boots on a bed! Another ventured fully clothed into the river Ilen, preferring to run the risk – very slight – of drowning to being found on a licensed premises on a Sunday. I was hidden in a large kitchen safe where I remained until the Guards put their notebooks away and went off to face the other evildoers of those distant days, the 'unlighted cyclists'.

The school-year began with a visit from the bishop whom I had previously seen in the Turkish Baths in Cork, though there was little to link the small, rotund figure wrapped in the folds of Turkish towelling with the dignified visitor from the episcopal palace.

Rumours were even then beginning to circulate that he might well be the last bishop of a diocese whose historic boundaries were those of the O'Driscolls. Being part of the diocese of Cork had no appeal for a people whose ancestors had sent their bishop to represent them at the Council of Trent, and Bishop Casey is known to have withstood efforts to convert him to the idea of amalgamation. His successor, Bishop Moynihan, was transferred to Kerry in 1954 and so, after eight hundred years of separate existence, Ross became an appendage of the diocese of Cork. An interesting feature of the amalgamation was that the then Bishop of Cork, Dr Lucey, was a stout opponent of centralizing power. He had opposed the closing down of creameries, post offices and police barracks in rural areas and had even intervened personally to prevent the amalgamation of national schools. The decision, however, rested with Rome and the eleven parishes of Ross* came under his jurisdiction and, despite spasmodic protests, have remained part of the Cork diocese.

St Fachtna's was then a small school and I had no more than nine in my Matriculation English class. The level of intelligence was high and many of the pupils even in Third Year Intermediate would take the examination for Writing Assistants in the British navy. In those early years the range of subjects was limited and I do not think that Science was taught. On the other hand almost every boy took Latin, and both Commerce and Drawing were on the curriculum. Classes ended at 3.30 p.m. with a half-day on Saturday at 1 o'clock.

My departure from St Fachtna's in the summer of 1939 was prompted more by a desire to take up a post at Lota on the outskirts of Cork city than by any dissatisfaction with life in Skibbereen. It was then, and possibly still is, a

---

*The eleven parishes were: Skibbereen, Castlehaven, Aughadown, Ardfield and Rathbarry, Barryroe, Clonakilty and Darrara, Kilmacabea, Kilmeen, Rath and the Islands, Rosscarbery and Lisavaird, Timoleague and Clogagh.

marvellously gregarious place. No one ever alighted from a train there unnoticed, no one was ever born or died there unrecorded. It is a friendly, talkative town with no need of a town crier or a gossip columnist. Nor is it all that difficult to conduct a conversation across the street even if traffic does at times cause an unwelcome interruption. Much of the talk has an extravagant boastfulness as when P. J. O'Sullivan, a well-known figure in the town in the 'thirties, challenged a Clonakilty rival to a score of bowls in order to prove that he, O'Sullivan, was 'the greatest man of this or any generation'.

Yet there always seemed to be unrest, even turbulence, underlying the surface gaiety, a smouldering awareness of some inner energy which seemed to find expression only when they left 'old Skibbereen'. This may in part be due to an ethnic richness which is not to be found elsewhere, a pluralism not only of stock but of religious sects. Where else in Ireland, within the confines of a few parishes, will you come upon such a variety of names as Camier and Caverley, Dukelow and Chudleigh, Swanton and Salter? Edith Somerville may have got it right when, in a letter of 1894 to her cousin Martin Ross, she wrote, 'I see that one day the Skibbereen district will be a fifth province of Ireland – refusing to receive home rule, and governed by Aylmer,* under a special warrant from the Queen.'

* * *

No inspectors, no syllabus, no curriculum, no time-table, no textbooks, no homework! A teacher's dream come true.

---

*Master of the West Carbery Hunt.

For the realization of such a dream, I had to thank Hitler and the Second World War.

It happened that in 1939 soon after the outbreak of war, the Brothers of Charity in Chorley, Lancashire, were notified that the area in which their novitiate was situated was a possible danger zone. They decided to seek temporary refuge in Ireland and bought Lota House near Glanmire, County Cork. Although the interior is much altered, it is substantially the same house that Arthur Young looked upon in 1776 when in his *Tour of Ireland* he gave his impressions of its setting:

> On the north side of the river which is much better planted particularly at Lota, the ground rises in bold ascents, adorned with many beautifully situated country houses. The view of Lota is charming, a fine rising lawn from the water, with noble spreading woods reaching on each side, the house has a very pleasant front, with lawns shooting into the woods.

One of the changes made at Lota between the time of Young's visit to Cork and the coming of the Brothers was the placing in the Venetian window at the head of the great double ramp staircase of the armorial bearings of the Crowley family, the last private owners of the house.

Having purchased the house, the Brothers advertised for a teacher of the novices. I applied and was appointed sole master of fourteen young men ranging in age from fifteen to eighteen.

Thus began a year in which I exercised an authority that Keate of Eton or Arnold of Rugby might have envied. And unlike them, I had no interfering governors and no importunate parents to trouble my days. The Brother Superior was fully occupied in laying the foundations of what has since become a residential home and school for moderately and severely handicapped children.*

On my first meeting with my pupils, we decided against having any textbooks and also that we would arrange in advance what subject was to be studied each day. Thus, we might decide to devote a whole day to Latin or divide the day in two and study English in one half and History in the other. When the sun shone, we emerged on the terrace fronting the house and went through a series of movements which would have shamed geriatrics. This we referred to as Physical Training! On summer days we walked down the front drive, crossed the main Cork/Waterford road and entered the grounds of Inchera where we had permission to swim.

It was a year of unalloyed joy. With the spectre of examinations banished, learning became a shared activity. A well-stocked library was our greatest resource and this we plundered for its treasures. What it yielded was not measurable, but I like to think that it was of enduring value.

As 1940 came and the German threat of invasion receded, my pupils returned to Chorley and I returned to a scrutiny of 'Situations Vacant'. I also entered my name on the books of two long-established London agencies,

*The work of the Brothers who devote their lives to the less fortunate gives to such places as Lota an air of remoteness from reality but there is nothing unreal in the dedication which they show towards those unable, in many cases, to do anything for themselves. They radiate cheerfulness, they make light of the most unpleasant tasks, they work unbelievably long hours, their patience seems inexhaustible. There is no need to go on. Lota is a place where life is made use of to count the gifts that life distributes in ways which can never seem fair to our limited intelligence.

Gabbitas and Thring, and Truman and Knightley. Graham Greene mentions these in his autobiography *A Sort of Life* and remarks that having recourse to them was rather 'like recourse to the pawnshop in earlier days'. I found them excellent in that they sent me long lists of schools bereft of teachers who by that time, the second year of the war, were mostly in uniform. However, before I was compelled to take the emigrant ship, a vacancy occurred in St Kieran's College, Kilkenny, to which I was appointed.

FOUR

St Kieran's — Glenstal — Scoil Éanna

FEW SECOND-LEVEL TEACHERS today enjoy the luxury of turning down offers of permanent, pensionable employment. I did during that summer of 1939 when vacancies occurred because of the call-up of teachers in Britain for service in the armed forces and the attraction at that time of the higher salary scales there. However, I was to learn that one can be too selective in a choice of school and it was already late September 1940 when, after an interview with the president, I was appointed to St Kieran's College, Kilkenny.

Few schools in Ireland have been so extensively written about as St Kieran's College. This in great measure is due to the Reverend Peter Birch who, long before he became Bishop of Ossory, wrote the history of the college. While I knew him as a teacher of English in the college, and many knew him as Professor of Education in Maynooth, it is as a social reformer that he is best remembered.

When I arrived there the college was one hundred and fifty-eight years old. The motto of the college, '*hiems transiit*, 1782', points to relaxation of the penal laws in that year. Winter had indeed passed for both teacher and taught.

One of the first matters that anyone coming to live in a strange town has to attend to is the question of lodgings. I was recommended to a house in Vicar Street beneath the shadow of St Canice's Cathedral. It proved to be an excellent choice and I can recall the laughter at the luncheon table in the college when the president, Father Ryan, asked me where I had found 'digs'. It so happened that my landlady had four extremely good-looking daughters, none of whom was married.

My stay in the college coincided with a period when there were some outstanding characters on the staff. Foremost among them I would put Peter Byrne. Peter wore broad-brimmed hats in the style of G. K. Chesterton, whom he resembled in bulk. A delightful raconteur, he was equally welcome at Kilkenny Castle and in the Workingmen's Club. He had joined the staff in the early 1900s and had left to take up a position as censor during the First World War before returning to St Kieran's in 1919. He spoke half a dozen languages and informed me quite solemnly during our first meeting that, like a famous Roman emperor, he spoke French to his wife, Italian to his mistress and German to his horse. I was later to learn that none of these was among his possessions.

He was on the staff when in 1910 three inspectors, Wright, Ensor and O'Neill, visited the college on 'General Inspection'. In their report they commented on the presence of the president of the college, the Dean of Studies, and the form teacher in the classroom during the inspection, 'a combination of terrors which would have made many of the older classes speechless with fright'.

One of my duties was to take the 'Ecclesiastics' once a week and read the gospels in Irish with those who were in their final year before ordination. The grave demeanour of those students, most of whom were older than I was, who stood up on my entry and remained standing until I had reached the rostrum, did much for my *amour propre*. The same students gave a rollicking performance of Goldsmith's *She Stoops to Conquer* on St Patrick's night, 1941, when I, in error, sat down in the chair reserved for His Lordship, The Most Reverend Patrick Collier, Bishop of Ossory.

At that time the college had some two hundred lay students and over one hundred ecclesiastics. The religious on the teaching staff varied constantly as is the way in all diocesan colleges, and in that year, 1940-41, there were fourteen priests and five lay teachers. This meant that the pupils met with teachers of widely different attainments often employing widely different methods for teaching the same subject. What was not different was discipline. In all classes I thought it stern to the point of severity.

It may not have been an excessively arduous life for the newly ordained clerics but for many it must have been frustrating and boring. 'Frustrating' because it cannot have fulfilled their hopes when ordained, 'boring' because it could continue indefinitely and, given the longevity of parish priests in Ireland, it often did. A priest in a diocesan college may enter college as a boarder at the age of twelve, remain on after the age of seventeen or eighteen as a clerical student and, after ordination, continue to live within the walls of the college until released by the bishop to take up a curacy. Not all of them, like Peter Birch, can hope to become bishops.

I liked Kilkenny and yet left it unlamenting. A most pleasant place for the visitor but less so for he who seeks to settle there, and Kilkenny people always struck me as being well content with themselves, satisfied that others find much to envy in its racial and ethnic richness. That complacency and a certain mellowness is part of Kilkenny's heritage, together with old buildings and old traditions. It is an Irish town that is also a city with a long and varied history. It has never forgotten that great figures, military and ecclesiastical, passed through it, that parliament sat there and that it is today the seat of two bishoprics.

* * *

As Kilkenny was not an incremental post I left it in June 1941 and joined the staff of Glenstal School in County Limerick. It was understood that I would be taking Latin and Science, and help with junior tennis.

Now, to use the jargon of the present, it was not my scene at all. I was flunked in Latin in each of my university years and had come to know Hubert Treston, the Classics professor at UCC, quite well because of our frequent meetings at *vivas* which, having failed in summer, I had to repeat in autumn. Of Science I knew considerably less. Mr O'Reilly, who taught Science at Presentation College, had forcibly ejected me from the laboratory and had then made it clear to the superior that not even Galileo could teach me Science. As for my tennis, the computer has not yet been made which shows my ranking.

All schools begin the school-year in different ways. Glenstal began at Kingsbridge Station and for the Cork contingent at the Glanmire Station in Cork. As the south-bound train usually pulled out about 6 o'clock in the evening, groups gathered on the platform from 5.30 p.m. on. Boys, varying in height and shape and age, tried to affect complete unconcern as anxious parents fussed about them, straightening ties and smoothening unruly hair. Oddly enough, though thoroughly ashamed of parental attentions, they kept their distance from one another as if delaying the moment when classrooms and dormitories would take over from home.

The ultimate in shame was to appear on the platform wearing the school colours. There were of course schools that flaunted theirs, one in particular favouring a violent purple. Such displays were not for Glenstal whose subdued pink and grey might, so the laws governing such matters decreed, be worn at football matches in Limerick. Mercifully, the school seemed never to have insisted on caps.

Glenstal is in a beautiful setting in the quiet countryside of east Limerick to which the presence of the monks adds an air of never-changing serenity. It was then a small school of ninety pupils, many of whom seemed to have a remarkable capacity for indolence. Those of the lay staff who were not married lived in what to the local people was always called 'the castle'. And the towers and turrets, crenellated walls and vaulted ceilings, ministered to the feeling that we were indeed living in a medieval castle. It was, in fact, built in 1838 by Matthew Barrington, a solicitor with an extensive practice on the Munster circuit and who later became Crown prosecutor for Munster.

The family had long links with the county and Barrington's Hospital owes its foundation to Matthew's father who had a town house beside the Abbey river in Limerick city. Tragedy befell the family when Winifred, the only daughter of Sir Charles Barrington, was killed accidentally in an ambush on a car in which she was travelling in the summer of 1921. The East Limerick Brigade of the IRA had warned Sir Charles by letter that his daughter was keeping company with District-Inspector Captain Briggs and that it could not be held responsible if, in an attack on Briggs, she was injured. No inquest was held on either Briggs or Miss Barrington, and the military court which inquired into the circumstances of the ambush made no mention of the warning letter.

One reminder of the old days and of the power exercised even by the most benevolent of landowners is the existence of but one public house in the nearby village of Murrow, a stipulation dating back to the time when the village was part of the estate.

The headmaster of Glenstal, Father Mathew Dillon, had guided its fortunes from the time of its foundation as a small preparatory school in 1932. He was a man of strong views, notably on the need to teach Latin and the even more urgent need to end the obligation to teach Irish. Nor was he, during the war years of 1939-45, determinedly neutral. Classes were certainly suspended on at least one occasion during my stay in the school to enable pupils to listen to a broadcast by Winston Churchill.

His dislike of the Intermediate Certificate was based on his well-founded belief that it distorted a boy's view of education at too early an age. While he saw to it that all pupils were given the best possible preparation, high marks in an examination failed to impress him. He was more concerned with developing the character of those confided to his care and in that he was, I think, successful.

In the 'forties, when school grants from the State were given on a scale that would have made Scrooge seem generous, most headmasters sought economic stability before educational reform. Father Mathew made Glenstal one of the most enlightened schools in the country without sacrificing that stability. It cannot have been easy. Departments of Education in Ireland as elsewhere give grants only to schools which conform to rules laid down by the State, and 'conforming' means, in education as in all else, death to the non-conformist. It was against the suppression of individual qualities, under a system in which almost all schools taught the same subjects, that Father Mathew rebelled. He encouraged his pupils to develop interests which were not always directly related to the subjects on the curriculum of the Department of Education but which served to form the complete man.

His own words reveal something of his aims:

> We must try to produce a boy who will be as like as possible to what Christ would have been if He had chosen to be born into this environment. It is not, I think, impossible to imagine Christ in the world today as a working boy, as a schoolboy, as a young university student, and our idea of Him in these surroundings must be the ideal towards which we direct our efforts.

One of his most stoutly held beliefs was that the best teachers were rarely successful 'examination teachers'. By that he meant that the sympathetic, imaginative teacher was often hampered by the need to follow the syllabus laid down for the certificate examinations. He must have raised the blood-pressure of officials in the Department of Education to a dangerous level when he insisted that I was teaching a class even when I had but one pupil!

He also maintained that certain subjects were not suited to the school system and should not be examined. English

Literature was one and Art another. (He would I am sure also have included Music but I do not remember having ever discussed this with him.) To attempt to examine a subject in which the feelings of the individual are what matter most was not, he held, possible.

My years in that school were most enjoyable even if my teaching, as indicated, was not strikingly successful. First of all, I was never intended by an omniscient God to teach Physics. That simple statement embodies the truth that even if an orchard-full of apples fell on my head, I would never deduce the law of gravity or, indeed, any other law. Nor could anyone, no matter how gifted, ever convince me that an elephant weighed in air differed in some way from the same beast, i.e. from itself, when weighed in water. Chemistry, with its cabalistic signs and formulae, was even more unacceptable to me.

It cannot be said that my Science classes were exactly unpopular. On the contrary, the boys revelled in the unexpectedness, the unpredictability of it all. Buckets of water, sand and fire-extinguishers made their appearance at the door of the laboratory wherein and whenever I was conducting experiments. Clouds of chlorine-impregnated steam and the occasional explosion were often the signal for the end of the lesson which was followed by shouts of '*Sauve qui peut*' from the more historically conscious pupils.

Signs of academic effort were hard to come by in the Glenstal of my day. The pupils accepted that the existence of a school presupposes some attempt at study and, while they did not scorn scholarship, they made it clear that it was not for them. Their general attitude was well summed up when I was attempting to drum up some enthusiasm for irregular verbs only to be stopped suddenly by a laconic request that they might be permitted to listen to Joe Loss and his Band.

There are few schools which I recall with more affection, and I knew few greater joys than that of returning to the heart of the tranquil countryside beside the Mulcair river. It holds rich memories for me: hurling with the Murroe team, fishing at Barrington's Bridge, picnicking in the Clare Glens or watching a cricket match from the Tower

> As the run-stealers flicker to and fro,
> To and fro.

There is an unchanging quality about life in a monastery which communicates itself even to a lay man living on the fringe. The bells that each day mark the passing hours and alternate work and prayer, prayer and work: 'Chaque jour est pareil à l'autre, chaque année comme celle qui le précedait et ainsi jusqu'à la mort.' So it is in Clairvaux, in Maredsous, so it was in Mount St Benedict and so, doubtless, it will be wherever the monks settle and devote themselves to a life of work and prayer.

The school has doubled in numbers since the days when, in order to field a team to play in the Limerick hockey league, the boys had to 'borrow' one or two members of the staff. This increase in numbers seems not in any way to have altered the ethos of the school. Certain schools, particularly boarding schools, have a particular atmosphere and, in this respect, Glenstal does have an almost perceptible aroma of confidence. I thought of writing 'superiority' and rejected it because the whole life of the community is so simple. It has always seemed to me when watching a monk setting off to cut timber or milk cows, that the life differs little from what it was when Matthew Barrington lived here one hundred and fifty years ago.

What then has created the impression that Glenstal is somehow the Eton of Ireland? First of all, such an impression is false because there is no basis for it, but the label is there and it has stuck. The entry is, admittedly, selective but so is that of many schools. Fees are high but so are those of many schools. There was and, for all I know, may still be an excessive interest in games, especially rugby, but then obsession with sport is all too typical of many schools.

Glenstal Abbey School is determindly facing the very real difficulty that the years to come may pose for fee-paying schools under religious control. Its size, shape, philosophy and future development has been the subject of much discussion within the monastery during the past ten years.

What emerges clearly from these discussions is that the monks have chosen to direct their apostolate to the education of the rich. This they justify on the grounds that it is better 'to provide "education" for even a privileged few than to provide it for no one at all'. They are, however, determined to repudiate the notion that pupils seeking admission should be white, male, catholic and be able to afford at least £3000 p.a.'.

Changes in admissions policy will be accompanied by changes in the programme of studies. It has never been a school in which the Arts and the Humanities were cultivated, and it is now proposed to balance these by the introduction of more sternly practical subjects. The administrative and domestic arrangements such as cooking, gardening and, in general, what are essentially business matters, will be made part of the educational programme.

I left Glenstal because of certain sharp differences of

opinion between the headmaster and myself, differences, I may add, which time erased. These differences concerned our respective interpretation of particular phases of Irish history. At the time I felt a certain sympathy for that fictitious teacher of history who steadfastly refused to teach that Malachi had stolen a collar of gold 'from the proud invader'. His refusal was based on the belief that to recall an incident of the late tenth century – memories of which were possibly somewhat blurred – could only cause distress to the surviving relatives of the king!

* * *

When schools re-opened in September 1943 I was in a school which in every way was the opposite of Glenstal. It was Árd-Scoil Éanna founded in 1939 by Séamus Ó Broin, a man who merits the grateful remembrance of many teachers. He had begun life as a teacher with Pearse in Rathfarnham and when Coláiste Éanna closed he opened his own co-educational school in St Agnes's Park before buying Franshaw House at the top of Crumlin Road, Dublin.

It has prospered and today, with his daughter Reiltín as principal, it continues in the tradition which he established. It is a school firmly based on the conviction that the native language is important for all who live and work within Ireland, and also that second-level should not be the exclusive privilege of the rich. The people of Crumlin have remained loyal to the school which has provided their children with a sound education for almost half a century and which, during all that time, never sent out an account.

I took Irish and History and even after an interval of forty-three years I can recall the enthusiasm with which those children embarked on simple projects which brought us to such places of historical interest as Kilmainham, Rathfarnham and, on one memorable occasion, to the Tolka river at low spring tide. The aim in each case was to vivify the history given in the textbook and this we most certainly achieved on the Tolka. We were re-enacting the battle of Clontarf and, having made our way from the North Circular Road in imaginary pursuit of the Danes fleeing before us, two of my charges sank to the waist in the mud below Binn's Bridge near Drumcondra. Had this happened in 1014 they may well have been forever lost, as we are told that the rising tide on that fateful Friday engulfed many of both victor and vanquished.

When I was there in 1943-44 it was a struggle to maintain numbers, as few children in a poor area such as Crumlin could be kept at school after the school-leaving age, which was then fourteen. Byrne's own words were that if a vacancy in another school was offered to a member of the staff he should accept, even if it meant having to drop the chalk and leave in the middle of a sentence.

FIVE

The Royal School — Kostka College

I LEFT SCOIL ÉANNA not in the middle of a sentence but in the middle of a term. It happened thus. In the early spring of 1944 I was in the office of the Association of Secondary Teachers (Ireland) then in South Frederick Street. While talking to the secretary, Florence Quirke, the telephone rang and as I went to leave the room, she motioned me to remain. I heard her assure someone that she would try to secure a teacher for him. The caller was the headmaster of The Royal School, Cavan. When she had finished I asked her permission to use the telephone. Minutes later I put down the receiver and told her that I had been appointed to the vacancy in Cavan.

I was perhaps more fortunate than Geoffrey Coulter, who was on his way to take up a position in the same school in 1924 when he met Peadar O'Donnell. 'You'd be lost teaching in a Protestant school in Cavan,' Peadar is said to have told him, and offered him instead the job of assistant editor of *An Phoblacht* at a pound a week. Geoffrey never went to Cavan.

'Cavan Royal', as it is usually known, is the oldest school in which I taught. (Kilkenny College is older but when offered a post there under the headmastership of Shankey, I had reluctantly to refuse as it was non-incremental.) The present headmaster, Douglas Anderson, is the twentieth to hold that office since 1611, when John Robinson was invested with the title during the reign of James I. The school flourished under the Stuarts and there is a local tradition that James II stayed near Swellan on the night preceding the battle of the Boyne.

We know something of what life was like within the school two hundred years ago from a letter written by the headmaster, Dr Cottingham, to his friend Robert Marshall in Dublin Castle in 1788:

> The bell rings at seven in the morning in summer and at eight in winter to assemble the young gentlemen. Prayers are said and business goes on till nine when an hour is allowed for breakfast and amusement. At ten they assemble again and continue in school until three, when they are called to dress for dinner. The French and Writing masters spend the entire day in the school and in the evenings the Dancing Master attends. The times of vacation are the month of July and from the 21st of December to the latter end of January in each year.

The curriculum has changed since the days of the Dancing Master and even since the year 1910, when those indefatigable inspectors of the Intermediate Board, Ensor and Rea, seemed somewhat taken aback at the work being done in the Preparatory Grade. They found that the English lesson was on the Witenagemot and that the pupils were learning about 'wapentakes' and 'hundreds' while in the open an assistant master was taking a class in Musketry!

Nothing so bizarre was demanded of me, and I took Geography and French to all classes. The school is a mixed school and as I was replacing Miss McIlveen, I was boarded but did not live in. Accommodation was found for me at the gates of the school with a Mrs Galligan to whom I paid seven shillings and sixpence a week. The house in which I was lodged in College Street is easily identified as there is a plaque on the outside wall, not, I must add, to me but to 'Patrick Galligan, Merchant, Chairman Cavan Urban Council'.

The headmaster showed great restraint when, on my first night on duty, I inadvertently brought the boys to the girls' dormitory. A stairway led to a wide landing where without signs to guide me and, need I say, without any guidance from the boys, I led my troops in the wrong direction. Forty years later I found myself enjoying a play at the Barbican Theatre in London entitled *The Happiest Days of Your Life*, in which a rather similar scene is enacted. The plot of the play is based on a civil servant's error in billeting a girls' school on a boys' school during the Second World War.

The Reverend Anderson, in the best tradition of Anglo-Irish headmasters, kept a few hunters and one of these, Irish Bachelor, was entered for the spring meeting at Punchestown. It may seem odd to present-day racegoers for a horse to be walked to the racecourse, but Irish Bachelor was walked from the training stable in Mullingar to Punchestown. The explanation is that during 'The Emergency' petrol was almost unobtainable and racehorses, even when owned by Protestant clergymen, were not in the category of VIPs to whom a ration of petrol was available. In an excess of loyalty to an animal we had watched at exercise and often talked to in his box, we all presented varying sums of money to the local bookmaker praying him to accept them as evidence of the judgment of teachers in equine matters. The bookmaker, in common with others of his kind, graciously accepted our money and offered the generous odds of 5 to 1 against Irish Bachelor's winning. At the end of that April day his judgment was proved to be correct. Our horse was second.

I enjoyed my stay at 'The Royal' and even if few have ever rhapsodized over the beauty of the Kennypottel river which runs through or rather underneath the town, it has a measure of attraction. I have happy memories of swimming in Swellan lake behind the school and of cycling to Lough Erne with another teacher, Jim Hetherington, at weekends. Lough Erne was then a base for the Catalina and Sunderland flying-boats and it was possible to picnic at Castle Archdale and watch these aircraft as well as the twin-tailed Liberators coming in from the Atlantic along the narrow corridor between Donegal and Fermanagh.

* * *

My departure from Cavan was in part due to aircraft of a different kind. Aer Lingus was even then (1944) planning for the expected post-war expansion and, improbable as it now appears, I was for a brief period to become part of that programme of expansion. It happened that in the spring of 1944 the company advertised for Traffic Officers. I applied, and so imperfect were the selection procedures that I was accepted. I was measured for a uniform and, when suitably attired, presented myself to the manager of the Dublin office, Mr Gerry O'Riordan. I was given a 'float' of £10 and took up duty at 56 Upper O'Connell Street.

By autumn, that is some five months later, the travelling public, i.e. the four passengers to whom I had managed to sell tickets and, indeed, anyone who had the misfortune to deal with me when making counter inquiries, must have realized that if Aer Lingus was to prosper, I should be forced to resign. To have made a passenger, who was a director of the Irish Tourist Association, weigh himself when he was probably the only passenger (it was the time when de Haviland five-seaters were in service), charge him for excess baggage when, if he was so minded, he could have brought a suite of furniture, issue him with a three-monthly return ticket when he was coming back *three days* later, and fail to book him into the Adelphi Hotel in Liverpool when requested to do so, must have alerted them to the dangers consequent on retaining my services.

In the event, after I was sent to Shannon where, incidentally, I never saw an aeroplane, I sought an interview with Mr Twomey, the Operations Manager, and informed him of my intention to return to teaching. To his enduring credit, he managed to conceal the unbounded joy he must have felt on realizing that the single greatest barrier to aerial advance was now lifted and that, for Aer Lingus, the sky was indeed the limit.

* * *

This time I returned to Dublin and to a part of the city where much of my teaching life was to be spent. A school under lay control, dedicated to Stanislaus Kostka, had been opened at the junction of Seafield Road and Castle Avenue, Clontarf. I knew the place and liked it, so when a vacancy occurred for a teacher of Geography, I applied. I was successful and moved to 'digs' on Kincora Road on the first day of September 1944.

There are posts of Special Responsibility in almost all second-level schools today. While at Kostka College I occupied a post which could with accuracy have been described as a Post of Spiritual Responsibility. It may be that the headmaster, Louis Roden, detected signs of sanctity in my general deportment or, as is more likely, had learned that I was in digs beside the school and therefore near enough to be of service.

Whatever the reason, I was his choice to accompany the younger boys to confession on Saturday mornings. I usually set off on this penitential exercise to the accompaniment of barking dogs and the derisive comments of those whose parents had other duties for their offspring on Saturday mornings. Vernon Avenue seemed endless and the sight of St John's Church on the seafront was as welcome as Canterbury to Chaucer's pilgrims.

The nature of those youthful sins remains unknown but there was always much lighting of candles in the post-confessional period of prayer on which I insisted. Though small candles cost no more than one penny, candle-makers must have rejoiced at the enthusiasm for dripping wax shown by penitents who in those days filled the churches on Saturday mornings.

My stay at Kostka College was very brief as I had earlier in the year been in touch with the headmaster of Ballymena Academy, who now made me an extremely attractive offer to go North.

SIX

Ballymena Academy

'BRIEF LIFE HERE IS OUR PORTION', 'Awake to Righteousness not Sin', and 'And after this the Judgment' – these and other similar lighthearted slogans greated me as I wheeled my bicycle bearing a suitcase, an umbrella and a hurley from the railway station in Ballymena, County Antrim, to my lodgings with Mr and Mrs Glass in Greenmount Terrace. It was late September in the year 1944 and I was 'the new teacher in the Academy' then on the old site of Thomas Street.

Ballymena Academy, founded in 1828, owes a great deal to the Fullerton brothers, one of whom, William, was the headmaster when in 1910 two of the newly appointed inspectors of the Intermediate Board came to the school on 'general inspection'. They must have been pleasantly surprised to find that all the staff were qualified teachers, which was unusual at that time, and also that all had teaching experience outside the country. They were well satisfied with the work throughout the school, though Kerin remarked that some of the sentences in the essays of the Middle Grade pupils were written in a kind of 'Hampton Court Maze style'.

It is no exaggeration to say that the Fullertons helped largely to shape the Academy of today. From the time of his appointment in 1900 until he was succeeded by his brother thirty-four years later, William Fullerton watched it grow from an enrolment of seventy-two pupils to one of five hundred. My own headmaster, William Bell, told me that when he was doing a degree in University College, Galway (to which a number of Ulster students always went), there was a Fullerton in the college from Moneymore who claimed as an ancestor Jonathan Fullerton, one of the first four Fellows of Trinity College, Dublin.

Ballymena Academy must have been one of the first schools in these islands to admit girls, which it did in 1900. It has to be borne in mind that the Intermediate Education (Ireland) Act of 1878 as drafted in its original form made no provision for educating them at all, so that the decision to admit them on the same footing as boys was a radical one.

No one could be long in the North without remarking on the excellence of all the educational services. One example of this is the official attitude towards the Irish language. Under the Ministry's regulations, if I wished to teach Irish I was required to have Irish on my degree and to provide proof of having spent at least three months 'in the study of the language in a district where it is spoken'. Even such proof would entitle me to no more than provisional certification. The renewal of my certification depended on my spending a further period of six weeks in the study of the language, attending a course and passing any examination held at the end of the course.

This was the rule in Northern Ireland at a time when in the Irish Free State and, later, after it had been declared a Republic, no one cared whether you knew a word of the language, Irish or otherwise, that you proposed to teach. My own case will best illustrate the point. I did not take French at school or university. I knew nothing of French language or literature. I had never been in France. When a vacancy occurred in 1947 in a secondary school, recognized by the Department of Education, for a teacher of French and Mathematics, I applied and got the job. From that year until 1977, when I resigned to take up a position in Canada, no one questioned my qualifications even when I was taking Leaving Certificate Honours French. No one cared.

Yet during those years the Annual Report of the Department of Education, which for some years was published in Irish only, contained such consoling words for those teaching French and German as the following: 'Éiríonn leis na hoidí cursaí maithe léitheoireachta a dhéanamh agus san am céanna gan faillí a dhéanamh sa chaint ná san fhograíocht.'* In the same year to which those words referred, the Department was making sure that 'conversation and pronunciation was not neglected' by having this gem of a question on the Intermediate Certificate (French) paper:

> Indiquez la prononciation de
> *c* dans blanc, écume, garçon;
> *s* dans accès, chose, ours;
> *im* dans simple, immortel;
> *il* dans autel, portail, fils.

This unique method of ensuring that Irish schoolchildren had a knowledge of the subtleties of sound in the French

*Annual Report of the Department of Education, 1957-58, p.13.

language must have been considered satisfactory as it was not altered until 1969.

Not that my own role in promoting those same 'subtleties of sound' would have earned me any decoration from the French government. I decided that in furthering the language I should teach my class some French songs. To this end, I drew on my own limited repertoire. 'Auprès de ma blonde' etc., I remembered since my time in France and so with that I began. But at once I encountered an obstacle. How was that final line 'Auprès de ma blonde [accented], il fait beau dormir, dormir' to be rendered? It was too much to hope that I would escape censure if boys at an impressionable age were heard singing lustily of such delights. So, should you hear anyone singing that well-known song with, as the final chorus, 'Auprès de ma grand'mère il fait beau dormir', you will know at once who his teacher was! As the French might say, 'Quelle délicatesse.'

The room I occupied in Ballymena was at the rear of the house, overlooking rooftops, outhouses and clothes-lines with, as a backdrop, the faint outline of Slemish mountain. On that first day I went to the post office to get the coupons necessary for survival in a part of Ireland severely hit by war shortages. Slogans of a different kind were in the post office: 'Talk can be Dangerous', 'Someone may be Listening'. When night fell, I had to accustom myself to the blackout, to the eerie blue of the occasional street lamp, to thin shafts of light where doors opened on darkened streets.

I choked back my nationalist sentiments when I went to take the obligatory Oath of Allegiance before Mr Henry, a local hotel-owner and magistrate. I filled in a form at the local RUC barracks which entitled me to a residence permit. I stood to attention in the Assembly Hall of the Academy for the British national anthem on the first day of term. I conformed.

Having been long accustomed to more leisurely ways in my previous schools, I found that life at the Academy was both real and earnest. Even when, much later in the term, the snow was deep and crisp and even, as I trudged slowly up the steps of the school the headmaster was waiting there to say, 'Nine o'clock and not five minutes past is the time for class.' No concessions to effete Southerners! I had approximately six hours of class on each of five days and on Saturdays I travelled with the Medallion (under fifteen) rugby team to venues in many parts of the North. My report of the result, together with any observations on the conduct of the players, had to be with Bob Mitchell, who took Games in addition to teaching History, on Monday morning.

While I am, as one of modest disposition, loath to take credit for it, two of that team did become internationals – Joe Gaston and Robin Gregg.

There were many compensations for the weeks of fairly unremitting work with Junior and Senior Certificate English classes. The countryside outside the town was beautiful, especially beside the Braid, and at the end of the first term I moved to a bungalow at Tullygarley within a field's distance of the river. There I stayed with the Adams family who were proud that on the father's side they were descended from the MacConnells who took part in the Rising-Out of '98. And I am grateful to my landlord, John Adams, who taught me to sing 'the Sash', as he said, just in case!

Another Presbyterian family, the Youngs, long associated with the language movement, lived nearby in Galgorm Castle, and Rose Young or Rós Ní hÓgain as she preferred to be called, was an aunt of the present Lady Brookeborough. Roger Casement, while a pupil at the Academy, stayed with his two aunts on the same road. A few miles outside the town lived Captain Jack White, one of the founders of the Irish Citizen Army: abundant evidence that Irish nationalism was limited neither by religion nor race.

Echoes of the past that have little to do with nationalism are not lacking in the town. The principal hotel, the Adair Arms, and Waveney, the name of a street, a terrace of houses and a licensed premises, are associated with one Robert Alexander Shafto Adair. He lived in Ballymena Castle and, writing of him in *Ulster*, Hugh Shearman tells how 'he had contested – I think – sixteen elections unsuccessfully in the Liberal interest, and when he was actually returned to Parliament at last, he lost his seat again in a fortnight as the result of a dissolution of Parliament; so Mr Gladstone advised Her Majesty to reward or console Sir Shafto Adair with a peerage'* which he did in 1873, making him Baron Waveney.

Beyond Galgorm where the road turns towards Ahoghill, the fief of Lord O'Neill, is the little Moravian settlement of Gracehill. There the members of what is possibly the oldest Protestant Church in Europe worship in a small church set in the middle of their own graveyard. It is a quiet part of the world, so quiet that I used on winter evenings to leave my bicycle by the roadside and then jog for two or three miles before returning. That was during the war when, alas, there were no Olympic Games where my athletic efforts might have been rewarded.

---

*Hugh Shearman, *Ulster*, (London, 1949) p. 276.

Ballymena is a town of which it has maliciously been said that the inhabitants worship property, profit and privilege. I never found it so but I did feel that there was an assumption among sections of the population that virtue should be revealed and vice concealed. Whenever I was invited by a Presbyterian friend to go for a drink, we did not enter the bar by the front door but by a side door. This, my friend explained, was to safeguard me, a teacher in the Academy, from evil tongues.*

Apropos the liquor trade, I knew of but one public house in the town that was not in the hands of a Catholic. That was in Linenhall Street and the owner later emigrated to New Zealand. Easily the most quaint and old-fashioned bar was that of James McKendry in Broughshane Street. What his politics were I can only surmise but I have a memory of seeing him standing at the door of the bar on VE-Day when the street was aflame with Union Jacks. No flag fluttered from his premises. Had the Allied victory no message for him? Or was freedom, as he saw it, still as far away as on the other summer's day when King James fled from the Boyne?

At the end of the first term there was a very prim and proper concert in the Assembly Hall. That evening a group of us, all teachers, went to a dance in Straide Orange Hall. Never a particularly gifted dancer, I was completely lost in a maze of schottisches, quadrilles, mazurkas and what may have been Highland Flings. I might have got through to supper-time but for a rash decision. I boldly asked out a local girl for 'The Grand Old Duke of York', an intricate

*Something of this determination to avoid giving scandal is shown in the life of Timothy Eaton, whose magnificent shopping centres are to be seen right across Canada. The range of goods on offer in his stores would appear to be limitless, but in none is alcohol sold.

measure calling for some smart footwork. I should have known better. Hardly had we begun to circle the floor than my partner said in a voice that could be heard in Cullybackey, 'You know nothing at all about it,' and abandoned me in the middle of the floor. That severed any loose connection I may have had with the Terpsichorean art. I have not since been seen on a dance-floor.

I had been in Ballymena for the best part of a year when the General Election of 1945 was declared. My landlady showed me the election manifesto of the Socialist Republican candidate for mid-Antrim, Captain Jack White. It was an odd choice of label for anyone seeking votes in the Braid valley, but White was never the man to fear the political and religious orthodoxies of Unionism. On impulse I wrote to him, disagreeing with points he had made, particularly in reference to the neutrality of the Irish Free State. Within days I had a reply and an invitation to dinner at Whitehall, Broughshane.

Anyone who ever met Jack White remembered him. It was not so much his commanding appearance, though someone standing 6 feet 3 inches has an advantage in that respect. Nor was it the voice, that had never entirely lost the very distinctive accent of his native Antrim. It was what Denis Ireland in an unforgettable phrase called 'the apocalyptic grandeur' of the man who had spent a lifetime fighting, and almost always *contra mundum*. The word 'fighting' is not misapplied; he had fought as a red-coated soldier in the Boer War, as a green-coated one in the Citizen Army, as a protester on picket lines in South Wales and as an ambulance driver in the First World War. He was a twentieth-century Don Quixote ever tilting at the windmills of imperialism and sectarianism.

For me to meet a rebel Protestant was something of a revelation. I had shown my dislike of the Northern regime by such feeble gestures as sulkily tendering my Residence Permit at the RUC Station when requested to do so and by absenting myself from school assembly on Empire Day. They were Lilliputian acts compared with the roaring defiance with which Captain White greeted the appearance of three members of the RUC in uniform when on a summer's evening in 1945 he opened his election campaign in the Orange Hall, Broughshane.

The constables had quietly climbed the wooden steps and, hoping to remain unobserved beside the big, cobweb-covered Lambeg drums, had stood there in the gathering dusk. In a voice that Pavarotti might have envied, White bade them not to skulk like rats but to come up to the front and sit like honest men where their faces could be seen.

That gathering in the upper room may have differed little in aims and aspirations from that of another June day in 1798 when rebel Protestants had marched down the Braid to join the insurgent leader, General James Dickey, at Tullymore. It was a Presbyterian clergyman, The Reverend R. Strawbridge, chairman of the Board of Governors of the Academy, who presided at the 1945 meeting, and it was another Presbyterian clergyman, The Reverend McSkimmin, who accompanied the pikemen of '98 on their way to Ballymena.

Jack White had not waited until 1945 to make known his opposition to what he considered to be the unnatural association of Protestantism with bigoted Unionism. He had much earlier in his career addressed the meeting in Ballymoney in October 1913 which proclaimed 'that Protestants of County Antrim are standing out to fight

Carsonism and proclaim their faith in a united Ireland'. That thread of nationalism persisted from 1798 through the days of The Reverend J. B. Armour of Ballymoney to that evening in 1945 Armour's hostility was directed largely against the Anglican Church and the landed classes, while White's venom was directed against the Orange Order which would separate working-class Catholic from working-class Protestant.

The other face of the North was shown not, as it happened, in County Antrim but in Dublin when on 19 November 1913 the Provost of Trinity College, Dr Anthony Traill from Bushmills, forbade the students of the college to attend a meeting of the Civic League. The meeting began in the Mansion House but because of the conditions under which they had been given the Mansion House, i.e. to maintain an attitude of neutrality on the trade dispute then going on, it was decided to move elsewhere. Then all in attendance, with Captain White and Professor R. M. Gwynn at the head, marched down Dawson Street to Trinity College. The night porter saluted Professor Gwynn and all passed through the Fellows' Garden to his rooms where the meeting was resumed. Captain White read a telegram from Sir Roger Casement expressing his support of a movement 'to drill and discipline Dublin workers' and a proposal to form a Citizen army of the strikers was unanimously adopted. That was the prelude to the more historic meeting held in March of the following year when a constitution for the Citizen Army, drawn up by Sean O'Casey, was ratified. The constitution affirmed that the Citizen Army would be 'open to all who accept the principle of equal rights and opportunities for the people of Ireland', and that one of its objects was 'to sink all differences of birth, property and creed under the common name of the Irish people'.

In his long and tempestuous life White's courage never failed, nor did his conviction that there was an alternative to the monolithic power of the Christian Churches which he saw as buttressing sectarian divisions. He remained close to the Presbyterian faith within which there was ever room for a robust tradition of dissent as well as vigorous theological dispute. This he welcomed even though he dissented from that religion's sense of elitism and supremacy. His was the dilemma that has faced Labour in Northern Ireland, and that still faces it, of trying to effect a balance between Nationalist and Unionist aspirations.

After that evening in Broughshane I was to meet Jack White but once more. Within months he was dead of cancer, leaving his wife, Noreen, and three sons to mourn him. Of Noreen he once wrote to me, 'Unlike your Church, I believe in the sincerity of my own marriage which to her is mortal sin and I have committed it twice, as she is my second Catholic wife.'

I will remember him not as he appears in the photograph of the Citizen Army taken outside Liberty Hall in 1913, or in the frontispiece to his semi-biographical novel entitled *Misfit*, but as I saw him riding through the streets of Ballymena on his grey horse. He usually came in on a Saturday when the streets were lively with the shouts of traders come from Belfast and Derry for the market and the noisy chatter of hundreds of Gibralterians evacuated from 'the Rock' for the duration of the war. What, I often wondered, were his thoughts on seeing the children of those over whom his father, Field-Marshal Sir George White, was once governor and among whom he lived until 1905 when he left for

India with his regiment?

My stay in Ballymena gave me at least some very slight idea of the complexity of thought that continues to baffle those seeking an understanding of life in a part of the province of Ulster: loyalists who refused to fly the Union Jack on V-Day but who, instead, flew the Red Hand of Ulster; Catholic school managers who refused to close their schools to permit pupils to harvest potatoes and so help the war effort; an academy wherein Casement was taught nothing of Ireland's history but where he heard the headmaster, Dr Robert King, speaking Irish to a beggar.

I said goodbye to the town of the Seven Towers and to its gentle hills – Knocklayd and Lurigethan, Trostan and Slemish – on a day in early July. The drummers had by then begun the season that would lead to 'the Twelfth', and the sound of the great Lambegs was already echoing menacingly through the province.

The Academy, whose motto is '*Tenax Propositi*', 'Steadfast of Purpose', remains to me the image of a school where there is certainly pride in past glories but equal pride in present achievements.

My decision to resign from the Academy was taken with one eye on the likely job position in Northern Ireland when the British army began demobilization and teachers would flood back to the classrooms they had left. I sent in my resignation by letter to Mr Bell on 30 April and, as it happened, he died suddenly a month later. The acting headmaster, Mr William Preston, kindly suggested that if I wished to withdraw my resignation I could do so, as no one knew whether Mr Bell had accepted it or not. However, my place on the incremental salary scale would suffer were I to remain in the North, so I returned to Dublin and began once again to consult the 'Situations Vacant: Education' column.

SEVEN

Wilson's Hospital — Headfort

ON AN AUGUST DAY IN 1945 I cycled the sixty miles that separated Cherryfield Avenue in Ranelagh from Multyfarnham, County Westmeath, for an interview with the Warden of Wilson's Hospital. The position advertised was for a teacher of French and English to Intermediate Certificate standard. The school had then no senior cycle and boys wanting to take the Leaving Certificate went to Mountjoy School in Dublin, as did boys from Kilkenny College.

The Warden, Canon Isaac Mayne, told me that I was the only applicant who had come by bicycle and after we had discussed conditions of work, etc. he offered me the position. I do not know if any conclusion can be drawn from his decision or if a sixty-mile cycle ride is any guarantee of success in the matter of appointments to the teaching profession. In fact, I really believe that the correct way to approach an old monastic settlement like Multyfarnham would be to don sandals and a habit of coarse hempen cloth tied with twine, and to carry a staff.

Before returning to Dublin I went down to Lough Derravaragh where the Children of Lir had spent three hundred years. Rooks cawed, sheep baaed, and in the distance a threshing machine throbbed. I felt that I was going to like Multyfarnham. I went into the Franciscan friary where Mícheál O Cléirigh, one of the Four Masters, worked in the seventeenth century and where for many centuries Nugents, Delamers and Cusacks had come to pray. The Nugents were Barons of Delvin and once owned much of the land between Multyfarnham and Mullingar, and in 1959 a fire demolished their great house at Donore.

The name 'Wilson's Hospital' may appear misleading until we recall that the public schools in England and the Charter schools in Ireland were originally charitable in intention. The King's Hospital in Dublin is the only other secondary school in Ireland which has retained this link with its original endowment. By the will of the founder, Andrew Wilson, dated 1724, lands were left in Westmeath for the building of a hospital not alone for 'Protestant male children but for aged men, being Protestant, and decayed housekeepers'.

The aged men and decayed housekeepers had long been forgotten when I arrived and even Protestant male children seemed in short supply. I had but five in my 4th Year (Intermediate) French class. All the pupils at that time were boarders with the exception of one of the O'Neills of Rathganny, who lived no more than a mile from the school. Numbers in most Protestant schools were then extremely low and Galway Grammar School had an advertisement in the *Irish Independent* giving the Leaving Certificate results, 'one entered, one passed'.

Wilson's Hospital had no secondary school boarders at all until 1898 when the nearby school of Farra,* one of the

*Memorialized by the Fermanagh novelist Shan F. Bullock in his autobiography *After Sixty Years* (1931).

many schools of the Incorporated Society for Promoting English Protestant Schools in Ireland, closed. The last headmaster, Dr Foster, was 'put to grass' where he seems to have browsed contentedly until 1939 when, in his ninetieth year, he died.

Farra had a rather picturesque setting above Bunbrosna, overlooking Lough Owel, and in its last year 'housed' twenty-eight foundation or free scholars and twelve pay pupils. With such small numbers it seems almost unbelievable that the school got to the final of the Leinster Senior rugby cup in 1886 and came close to beating Blackrock College in the final.

Canon Mayne's predecessors, The Reverend Hill Wilson White, and his eldest son, The Reverend Henry de Vere White, had presided over the destiny of Wilson's Hospital for sixty-six years. The author Terence de Vere White is a son of Frederick, a brother of The Reverend Henry. The long reign of Hill Wilson White and Harry White left the school in ritual and regime almost unchanged. Its physical appearance has probably remained unchanged for much longer. The oaken floors, tables and trestles, stone staircases and passages, inky desks with dates spanning more than a century, must be the same as those commented upon by the Royal Commissioners who reported on the school in 1812. The bathroom was certainly deserving of a listing as 'Early Antique' in any catalogue. When I last saw it, it contained two huge rust-encrusted baths each standing on four lion's paws. Thick flakes of enamel floated on the surface every time a bath was filled from taps which provided no more than a reluctant trickle of tepid, mud-coloured water. On bath-night the master on duty had to see to it that each pupil immersed himself at least once in this uninviting mixture. This task was usually performed with the aid of a brush. As there never was an inexhaustible supply of water, I saw to it that four went in at a time, the fatter ones tending to float on the surface like hippopotami.

The Commissioners of 1812 seem to have done their work thoroughly and they wound up with an intriguing comment in the Appendix to the General Report. In giving an account of the number of boys received into and apprenticed out of the school between the years 1789 and 1808, they mention thirty who 'eloped'. This, when I read it, set me thinking. Was it possible that boys of school-going age were romantically involved to the point of eloping? However, *The Shorter Oxford English Dictionary* does give 'to run away' as an equivalent meaning for 'elope' and so I take it that those nineteenth-century schoolboys had done just that.

In my year quite a few scampered off into the night during the first weeks of term, victims of homesickness rather than of love! Their flight was usually timed for after supper on a moonless night. This meant that pursuit was rendered difficult when, after the 9 p.m. roll-call, their absence was noted. Many chose to follow the railway line leading to Mullingar while others preferred the main road with its opportunities for 'lifts'.

Most of them returned or were rounded-up before midnight, given hot cocoa by the matron, Mrs Rose, and sent to bed. Discipline was never harsh and the Warden himself was a kindly man, much in the tradition of country parsons whom we know about from novels and imagine when we see 'The Vicarage' on pillars of a solid country house. He was a big, broad-shouldered man who easily assumed a sort of Roman *gravitas* when, at the beginning of the school-year, he addressed the boys. On one of these occasions we were listening to him through a hatch in the Common Room. You may imagine our chagrin when we heard him announce somewhat apologetically that while he had done his best to secure good teachers to fill the vacancies on his staff, he had found it difficult to do so and the best would have to be made of those he had employed!

The income from the 180-acre farm attached to the school was an important factor in keeping fees low. The farm steward in my time was Mr Dickson. He was tall and angular with long, carefully-waxed moustaches that stretched to either side of his face like the horns of highland cattle. He was a man of few words but invariably prepared to predict rain at all seasons of the year. When questioned on the weather he nodded his head up and down, and this deliberative gesture had won him a reputation for sagacity far beyond the bounds of the school. Other than the weather, he had but one subject of conversation. This was the crimes perpetrated by greenfly and caterpillars, but few who listened to him on this topic would have preferred it to the weather. To see him in knee-breeches and leggings, leaning on a gate surveying his flocks and herds, was to think of Farmer Oak in Hardy's *Far from the Madding Crowd*.

Like most of the staff, I lived in. The only married teacher among us was Mervyn Morrow and he lived in one of the many buildings which formed part of the central courtyard. It wasn't that the rest of us had taken vows of celibacy or anything like that. Rather was it that salary scales offered little inducement to change. Matrimonial delights, as we imagined them, paled when set against the marvellously restful life of a resident teacher in a school where 'examination pressure' was unknown. I spent many autumn days during that first term within the four-acre walled garden with the school cat, Clarissa, for company and nothing to disturb the silence but the petals falling from the rose bushes and the murmur of pigeons in the beech trees on the back avenue.

Those pigeons led much less restful lives. Both Mervyn Morrow and Eric Shier were happy to supplement their teacher salaries by selling pigeons at three shillings and sixpence to Associated Merchandise in Dublin, and more than the dodo would by now be extinct were cartridges more readily available in those post-war times. Despite what some sporting purists may say, these two teachers had discovered that the most efficient way to end the life-cycle of a pigeon was while he sat contentedly under a tree chewing the beech-mast. What St Francis of Assisi would have thought of it all is not known, but in extenuation it could be claimed that the pigeons were Protestant.

Sometimes when I borrowed Mervyn's shot-gun in a half-hearted effort to reduce the rabbit population of County Westmeath, I was accompanied by another teacher who had joined the British army at the outset of the First World War but had never seen service at the front. His eyesight was not Grade I and it was generally agreed that if he were entrusted with a gun it might seriously imperil the lives of his fellow-soldiers. On one of our hunting expeditions he was carrying the gun, and when he sighted a rabbit he rested it on my shoulder and took careful aim. The rabbit I should explain was so near that we could hear it munching. With a whispered warning to me not to stir, he fired. When the sound had died away beyond the woods of Clonhugh, we saw not one but two rabbits scampering off. 'Good God', he exclaimed, 'I've split him!'

Our sporting activities were not confined to bird and beast. We also 'stalked' the bream in nearby Lough Owel. Not for us the tedious tying of flies or the thrusting of worms on hooks. Rather was a dark night chosen when in waders we made our way up one of the feeder streams flowing into the lake. I can speak with first-hand knowledge of this nocturnal exercise as I was brought along, largely I think to carry the net-bag, on more than one occasion. It is an exciting moment when the fish, surprised by the sudden movement of hands through the gills, are thrown on to the bank. Such methods could hardly be expected to commend themselves to the local *gendarmerie*, and indeed an old man assured me that his grandfather had been 'transported' in the previous century for taking fish in such an unorthodox manner.

While bream are best in early spring when frost is still in the air and the nights sufficiently dark to offer concealment from inquisitive eyes, for trout we waited, like genuine licensed anglers, until the coming of the month of May. As soon as we got word from Jack Lynam or Frank Gaynor of Mullingar that the mayfly were up, we pushed out the boat on Ennel or Sheelin, fished all day and cooked the catch on the hot embers of the fire in the Common Room. Our culinary methods were extremely simple: we wrapped each fish in well-soaked layers of brown paper and when the last layer was completely charred we knew the fish was cooked. If the mayfly did not rise, we fished for perch at the White Lake beyond Castlepollard. These we filletted and then dipped in flour, pepper and salt before frying on a fire which was well fed with beech logs.

When the first warm days came, a task force was sent out to prepare a wicket in one of the fields fronting the school. When the boys had completed the work, regardless of weather the cricket season opened. I had to take a lot of cricket probably because I had not taken rugby during the winter. It was my custom to go in to bat when practice began and to remain at the wicket until the bell rang for 'prep'. I also took all the bowling and ignored the convention in accordance with which the field changed with each over. In the face of my inflexible determination to keep on batting regardless of whether the stumps fell or the bails flew, the pupils developed self-restraint and at the same time gained wide experience in the arts of bowling, wicket-keeping and fielding. As no umpires were needed, there were none of those languid interruptions signalling 'Over up', none of those frequent shouts of 'Howzat', and none of those outbursts of irritation when appeals are not upheld.

While the charge of being recusants could not be levelled against us, three of the staff including myself did not, let us say, subscribe to the Thirty-Nine Articles. Thus during the period allotted on the timetable to Religious Instruction, we usually made our way across the fields to witness the most exciting event of the rural day – the arrival of the Dublin train. We then followed the cart carrying the mailbags to the post office where the Misses Killian presided over the sorting and, some would say, the perusal of the mail. Returning across the fields heavy in summertime with rich grass, Paddy O'Kane, who had studied his Latin very thoroughly at Maynooth, was sometimes moved to quote Virgil. He would stand on a headland and to an audience of mystified cows would quote the lines beginning 'How blest beyond all blessings are farmers, if they but knew their happiness'!

To ensure that the school did not forget the decent

farmer, Andrew Wilson, to whom in great measure we owed our idyllic existence, a day was set aside every September to render thanks for his gift. In the school chapel, altar and lectern, font and choir stalls were garlanded with sheaves of corn and baskets of apples and vegetables, enough to delight the old farmer's heart. And, as the evening light faded, the choristers sang and we, the members of the staff, prayed with them for the rich to be impoverished, the proud to be humbled, and the mighty to be brought low. Finally, the entire congregation, many of them emitting sounds ill-suited to any hymn, Ancient or Modern, sang lustily 'O God Our Help in Ages Past' before separating for another year.

If I am to return to earth in any future incarnation, it will I hope be as a teacher in an unchanged Wilson's Hospital, for few places could assure such delights as were ours in the Midlands of forty years ago: boating on the Inny, picnicking at Crookedwood, swimming in Derravaragh. There may not have been a Lamborghini or a Ferrari between us but we did get around quite well in a 1936 Prefect belonging to Mr Connor. So well, indeed, that we may have been the teachers whom Captain Giles, TD for Westmeath-Longford, had in mind when on 13 June 1944 he spoke in Dáil Éireann on the Vote for the Department of Education:

> At the present moment we have a crazy system run by fanatics who do not know anything. They teach for five or six hours, then get out and have a good time afterwards. A good many teachers blow into my county from God knows where and do not seem to have any qualifications, but they go around the country as irresponsible fanatics night after night. You could not expect farmers or

labourers to send their children to schools where they were teaching.

Wilson's Hospital is today a prosperous, co-educational school, differing in many ways from that in which so many teachers laboured in the course of over two centuries. No longer is the Warden obliged to be a clergyman, so that Robert Whiteside, installed as Warden in 1985, will not, unlike Terence de Vere White's grandfather, Dr Hill Wilson White, be spending much of his time 'composing sermons and giving lessons in Greek to the ladies of the county'.

Four of us, O'Kane, Shier, Morrow and myself, handed in our notice to the headmaster on 30 April in that year 1946. It is quite difficult to give any over-all reason for such an exodus. Morrow decided to give up teaching, Shier went as senior master to a school in Antrim, O'Kane went as Classics master to the High School, Dublin, and I went back to my native Cork. This was a temporary appointment and by spring of the following year I was back in Dublin where I 'touched down' in a school for one day before going on to my fourth school in the space of one year'!

* * *

How I came to join the staff of a school and resign from the same school all within twenty-four hours requires some explanation. It happened that I was approached to do some substitute teaching in a national school on a day-to-day basis. I began in City Quay Boys' school at 9 a.m. and while reading the newspaper at lunchtime I saw an advertisement for a teacher at Headfort House near Kells, County Meath. I tendered my resignation and my apologies for such short notice to the headmaster, Mr Cawley, and at 3 p.m., when classes ended, telephoned Headfort House.

I spoke to the headmaster, Group-Captain Watkins, MC, DSO, and he, with an alacrity which convinced me that teachers must have been in short supply, agreed at once to my coming. He did, admittedly, question me as to my willingness to teach subjects likely to be offered for Trinity Entrance, take games and supervise study. He could, had he but known, have thrown in gardening, animal husbandry, maintenance of machinery, etc., and I would still have agreed to accept a position in the residence of a marquis, so strong is the element of snobbery in all true-born republicans.

Let me give you something of the background of a family whose magnificent house has become a school. In 1660 an English gentleman from Sussex named Thomas Taylor bought land in County Meath. So did many other English gentlemen of the time but not all of them prospered as did the Taylors, soon to become Taylours. A baronetcy in 1704 was followed by more exalted titles leading to the marquisate in 1800. Any historical inference drawn from the latter date is correct.

The family were good landlords which ensured that no agrarian troubles or tenant discontent troubled them. Their generosity towards the Roman Catholic community found expression in a gift of land in Kells as a site for the chapel and a gift of money for schools. This, I may add, has not been forgotten and when on a Sunday morning, Geoffrey, the 5th marquis, most of the *domestiques* and myself arrived for Mass, white-surpliced altarboys scampered from the sacristy to place hassocks under our knees.

Not that the family lacked a sizeable skeleton in that

traditional hiding-place for such reminders of the past – the cupboard. In 1804 the Marquis of Headfort was convicted of 'seducing and taking away' the wife of The Reverend Charles Massy of Summerhill, who was awarded £10,000 damages. All that was forgotten when, one hundred years later, the 4th Marquis brought the former Gaiety girl, Rosie Booth, as his bride to Headfort amid great rejoicing. She had begun life in Tipperary where she went to school in the convent of the Ursulines at Thurles. As an actress, she was introduced to London audiences by George Edwardes and made her name in a number of musical comedies, notably 'The Career Girl' and 'The Messenger Boy'.

To arrive on a bicycle and carrying a fibre suitcase at a country house which owed its design to George Semple and much of its interior beauty to the decorative work of Robert Adam and to paintings of Zucchi, seemed entirely wrong. As it was almost midnight when I arrived, having travelled from Cork that day, not too much attention was paid to me and my bicycle. As the present Marquis, Michael, was then at school in Stowe, I was accommodated in that part of the wing where the family slept. I had an enormous bed or rather catafalque of resplendent whiteness with a lamp set in white marble beside it. A bathroom, dressing-room and study completed the suite. Everything for the comfort of a secondary teacher!

My window looked out on the yew walk, one of the principal glories of the Headfort gardens which in 1931 had won for the Marquis three major awards of the Royal Horticultural Society. Giant red cedars, beech and oak lined the main approach to the house, which was screened from the farmyard by banks of rhododendrons then in their early summer splendour.

I did not meet the headmaster until after breakfast on the following morning. He proved to be a most congenial character who welcomed me much as I imagine one of Somerset Maugham's magistrates in some outpost of the Empire welcomed a new arrival from the Foreign Office. He took me aside on that first day and confided to me his belief that the secret of a successful school lay in good food, an absence of punishment and long holidays. Who was I to quarrel with such views!

Life for me began at 6.15 each morning when a housemaid knocked, entered, set my morning pot of tea with its monogrammed cosy on the bedside table, pulled back the curtains and ran my bath. The next item on the day's agenda, class at 7 a.m., did at first seem to call for swift industrial action. I need not have worried. In a school with a pupil-teacher ratio of 2½ to 1, no tribunal would have shown me much sympathy. There were in all but five pupils in the school – the Grogan brothers, Traill, Gillespie and Stuart.

It is not every teacher who can recall the names of each pupil in a school after an interval of forty years. Traill's grandfather had been Provost of Trinity and he was preparing to sit the entrance examination to that university, as was Gillespie. The others were attempting the Cambridge Locals.

There among the cherubs and the damask and the gilt of a beautiful room, with a sleeping Pekinese in a basket in one corner, I held my first class. Each class was in effect a tutorial and all ended at 1 o'clock. Even the knowledge that I had to take study each evening did nothing to mar the delights of life on that twelve-thousand-acre estate. Tea on the terrace at 4 o'clock came in a silver teapot, with a tiered cake-stand, two kinds of bread and butter, white and brown, cucumber sandwiches, scones and fruitcake. This was followed by what Elgy Gillespie once described as that 'savage and unprincipled game' – croquet.

Study which began at 8.15 p.m. often ended at least for one of the two senior pupils when a rose was thrown through the casement window of the study-hall. The rose was a signal from some female member of Lady Headfort's staff that she would appreciate a companion with whom to explore the Meath countryside, nowhere lovelier than on the upper reaches of the Blackwater.

There were days when Sultan, a black retriever, or Minou, a white Persian cat, would push open the classroom door and curl up happily beneath an empty desk. On sunny days peacocks spread their feathers as they pirouetted on the lawn, and when evening shadows lengthened owls drifted out of the cedars to rest like stone effigies on the roof surround and on the pillars of the front porch. It was altogether Arcadian, more suited to the shepherds and shepherdesses of another age than to the requirements of twentieth-century schooling. If there were no shepherds or shepherdesses, there were kitchen-maids and parlour-maids and housemaids, while out-of-doors there were gardeners and under-gardeners and a farm steward, Major Pat Thunder, to rule over his large cattle empire.

You will ask why I ever left that idyllic setting where pupils were wont to 'fleet the time as they did in the golden world' and where unpretentious academic effort and simple sport seemed wedded in such harmonious proportions? Alas, had I not interpreted as an invitation a rose intended for someone much younger, I might today still be part of the estate now estimated as worth two million pounds.

Headfort School is today in many ways different. It

could hardly have continued to survive as I knew it. In 1949 it was decided to turn it into a Preparatory School with, as its first headmaster, Romney Coles. He was succeeded by David Wild who remained until 1977 when Lingard Goulding took over, and by then it had also become co-educational. Yet in some respects it has not changed: there is still tea on the terrace; peacocks strut on the lawn and the same owls may, for all I know, glide above the cedars at night.

It is likely that Headfort House will always be a small school. There are now some eighty pupils aged from eight to fourteen and paying some £4000 per annum in fees. The estate is owned by B. J. Kruger, the Canadian industrialist, who has leased the house to the school as well as the sports fields and gardens.

Independent schools such as Headfort rely very much on the political stability and economic prosperity of the country. They are financially vulnerable in a way that State schools are not. Given that the curriculum chosen and the syllabus followed owe nothing to the Department of Education, it is but reasonable that the Department should not subsidise them. Yet they are of positive educational value. Without them there would be no choice for parents and all pupils would be processed in much the same manner. Independence of mind is most valuable in a democracy and I would like to see some formula worked out so that Departmental recognition would at least be given to qualified teachers in these schools.

My last memory of Headfort, and one that is likely to endure, is of the evening when the present Marquis returned from England where he was at school, packed us all into a 1921 Clyno and proceeded to hurtle round the estate at a speed expected only of Formula One drivers to the accompaniment of simulated cries of terror from the boys and at least one very genuine adult squeal.

EIGHT

Newbridge College

THE TRANSITION FROM the domain of a nobleman to a school founded by an order of priests who were so poor that they had to sell seven of their silver chalices, is not easily effected. Nothing in any teacher training course prepares one for such a change. However, in that summer of 1947 I put aside my copy of Debrett's *Peerage, Baronetcy, Knightage and Companionage* and for the next ten years had the *Summa Theologica* of St Thomas Aquinas, all sixty-one volumes, within reach as bedside reading. Anyone will tell you that I never read in bed!

I don't know how the boarders arrive at Newbridge College today but in the past to arrive there by train was, I think, the best of all ways. Bill O'Neill, the stationmaster, was always on the platform to ensure that any new boys, 'ellers' as they were called, were not left behind on the train. Jim was there from the college with his horse-drawn dray for the trunks and somewhere along the way, Charlie Callaghan would be met cycling along, wearing his green baize apron, to welcome all back for another term.

Newbridge is a town that almost closed down when the Royal Horse Artillery and the Royal Field Artillery withdrew in 1921. It was said at the time that a few thousand pounds would have bought the Main Street and it is true that the Town Commissioners, in dire straits for money, did sell off some two-storey houses which belonged to them for £75. It was the horses on the nearby Curragh that gave employment during the decade that ended only when Irish Ropes established a factory in the town in 1930 for the making of Tintawn.

The Curragh is a place of unusual attraction, especially on a summer morning. There can be few more pleasant sights than that great stretch of grassland when the first strings of horses are led out in early morning and waves of green plover wheel and curve above them. Some horses, well rugged up, walk slowly around, nodding their heads and pulling at bridles. Others move towards where the gallops for the day have been marked by furze bushes. The Curragh is a world apart. At the core of the life of each trainer, jockey, groom and stable-lad is the horse.

I have always thought the name 'Newbridge' fairly meaningless and during my first year in the town I sought to interest people in changing the name to 'Old Connell' or 'Conallmore', names historically associated with the land bounding the river Liffey. I was unsuccessful and not for the first time. I had also failed to persuade the parish priest of Newmarket-on-Fergus, Canon Hamilton, to sponsor a movement to revert to the older, and topographically accurate, *Coradh Caitlín*.

The entrance gates to the college bear the arms of the college and show an antlered stag carrying an image of the crucified Christ. The stag figures in the arms of the Eustace family whose gift of land enabled the Dominicans to establish themselves in Naas in 1356. The present college dates from 1852 and it would appear to have been for long a small and not particularly distinguished boarding school.

When Edward Ensor on inspectorial circuit visited Newbridge in November 1909 there were but forty pupils in the building of whom three were over nineteen! Ensor was not impressed either by the quality of the work or by the amenities, if such they could be called, of the school itself. He stated bluntly that 'the exercise books are dirty and untidy, and the exercises are corrected by the boys in class. Apparently no teacher ever looks at the boys' exercises, as they are often hopelessly wrong, and the corrections are nearly as often wrong as right'. On that 'bitter frosty morning' Ensor took the Middle Grade class into the study hall, 'the only room in the school premises that was warmed'.

Even if the college authorities were to have done nothing in the intervening years to improve the heating, the Second World War made its own contribution to the pupils' comfort. Between 1939 and 1945 a number of *Luftwaffe* aircrews had for various reasons made forced landings in the Irish Free State. They were interned on the Curragh but a very civilized parole system enabled them to visit such towns as Newbridge and Kildare, each within walking distance of the Curragh Camp. Charlie Callaghan decided to make use of them to build a weir on the river and to set up a hydro-electric plant in the millrace behind the college.

The Germans proved to be excellent workers and as the college also employed a number of girls, any linguistic barriers were quickly overcome. They also made a contribution to the cultural life of the locality as they sang under the baton of Josef Cuypers in the church choir and helped in a production of *Die Fledermaus*. Cuypers was also responsible for some highly professional productions of Gilbert and Sullivan operettas on the college stage. During his absence through illness in 1947, the pupils staged 'The Merchant of Venice' with the present deputy editor of *The Irish Times* in the role of Portia. The play ran for three days when it was withdrawn, as someone said, by popular request! The theatrical ambitions of the college now range far more widely, and 'Oklahoma' and 'South Pacific' have been performed in recent years.

The college doctor was Dr Joseph Roantree, whose association with the town as dispensary doctor spanned sixty-four years. He had been appointed in 1896 and as there was then no statutory retiral age, he simply went on and on. He attended me in 1950, and after climbing the six flights of stairs to my room beside the clock tower, he was scarcely out of breath.

I came to know him well after I had left the town and he had a fund of remarkable tales. His people were farmers in County Armagh and the men who sat by the kitchen fire in his father's house when he was a boy were veterans of Waterloo! The father of a gardener whom they employed had seen two of his schoolfellows lying dead on the battlefield of Ballinahinch in 1798. His own life had not been without incident, and during the severe winter of 1912 he did his rounds in a sleigh built by a carpenter in the town.

There are schools which see examinations as signposts that may be ignored at no great peril. The Dominican college, as I knew it, was one of these. The usual certificate examinations were taken but without any excessive enthusiasm, and the monthly visitation of the headmaster to each class did little to affright even the most timorous pupil. Father O'Beirne's strongest criticism was invariably accompanied by an admonition to the effect that socks needed to be pulled up and one's best foot needed to be put forward. Remarks, you will admit, unlikely to make hair stand on end.

The Newbridge system seems to work: the pupils pass their examinations, they do well in life whether in factory, field or the professions. They return willingly to the college – always a good sign – and, in many cases, send their children along as boarders. There is little talk among them of wishing to burn it to the ground, the wish of a not inconsiderable number of people when their old school is mentioned. In fact anyone who lived in the college, as I did, must have left it with some feeling of regret. While the aura of sanctity is not, or so I am told, immediately discernible even to those who look closely at me, I did like the cloistered quiet of the priory. Much of the community life became our life even if we lay teachers did not adhere too strictly to the canonical hours.

When the time to elect a new prior came round, as it did every three years, we did not hesitate to chalk up on the staff room mirror the odds on the various priestly candidates whom we considered to be in the running. And, although the finer points of the Thomist philosophy escaped us, nevertheless, we did set problems to the senior classes on the number of angels to be found on the head of a pin, given the diameter of the pin!

The painter Millet has evoked memories of the Angelus in his painting of that name. I have my own memory of the Angelus hour in that school beside the Lilffey. In my picture there is a man and his one cow. The man, Micky Donnelly, lived beside the college. Most evenings as he drove the cow back for milking, the Angelus rang from the college tower, whereupon Micky stopped, grasped the cow's tail and there the two remained motionless while Micky, with bent head, recited the prayer.

For a school which takes its rugby quite seriously, far too seriously, success has largely eluded it. I can remember celebrating but one triumph during my ten-year stay. That was the winning of the Leinster Junior Cup in 1950. The team was H. Murphy, M. Collins, F. Fallon, J. Delahunty, J. Fitzpatrick, T. Twomey, D. Colbert, B. Sweeney, T. Reid, R. Lawrence, D. Farnon, F. Conway, B. Rigney, J. Murray, S. Byrne. It was not of course always a rugby stronghold and in the early days of the GAA, St Thomas's College, as it then was, represented Kildare in the Leinster Senior hurling championship.

Motorists passing through Newbridge on their way south must think of it, as they might think of Newmarket or Aintree, as a racing centre – a scene of betting coups that failed, of dawn gallops watched through telescopic lens. For me it is the place where for the last time I lived in a boarding college. There are, I know, teachers who would not accept to 'live in'. I rather liked it. Certain almost feudal privileges went with it. Where else would I have my bed made, my room dusted, my shoes polished and a fire lighted in my room after I came up from breakfast on a winter's morning? In the late 'forties Newbridge College was ideal for the celibates of the staff, and there were five of us.

Having said all that, I must add that no boarding school, no matter how good, is any substitute for home. Yet in Ireland, where there would appear to be such emphasis on the Christian family and the home, thousands of boys and girls are herded away to be cared for by strangers. I have lived in four boarding schools and I claim to know something of the misery that is often the lot of those who at twelve years of age are separated from their parents. They will, of course, receive a weekly letter and food parcels by which parents seek to still any murmurings of conscience at what they have done. Parents will be heard to say 'It will toughen them' and then grumble if, in later years, their toughened children turn away from them.

A letter written over two hundred years ago gives in simple words an impression of what the life is like for some if not for all:

> My Dear Dear Mother
>
> If you don't let me come home, I die – I am all over ink, and my fine clothes have been spoilt. I have been tost in a blanket, and seen a ghost.
>
> I remain, my dear dear Mother,
>
> Your dutiful and most unhappy son,
>
> FREDDY
>
> P.S. Remember me to my Father.*

How boarding schools continue to survive at a time when parents are being criticized for abdicating their responsibilities is all very odd. It is certainly strange to find religious orders preserving a system which cannot fail to weaken parental authority. The claim that they cater for a need is not the answer. The onus of justification lies not in showing that boarding schools meet the children's needs but in showing that these needs can be met only by boarding schools and in no other way.

There are many flaws endemic in the boarding-school

*Frederick Reynolds, 1775, from *Westminster*, by J. D. Carleton.

system: an outmoded hierarchy of values linked to houses, prefects, merit awards; too little personal responsibility; excessive emphasis on one particular form of athletic activity. They served a purpose when education was rationed and restricted. That time is at an end and if we are to build an Ireland based on the mutual help and co-operation of communities, then the co-educational day school must be the foundation of our system of education.

Gerald Brenan said it all and said it well when he wrote in *A Life of One's Own*, 'If they are unhappy at their school, they will suffer despairingly, like prisoners who have been given a life sentence because they cannot imagine it ever ending.' Yet thousands of Irish boys and girls have gone to boarding schools and lived happily ever after. Psychologists call it survivor syndrome. Like the survivors of some terrible ordeal, they may pass several years in normal health but I maintain that it does leave some mark, some residue of those mornings when the shipper-in for the day goes through the dormitory rousing them from sleep.

It is necessary at this point to say that Newbridge College has drawn up a constitution for the future governance of the school which, to my mind, is of considerable educational significance.

The background to the change is that the school with its four hundred and fifty pupils, of whom one-third are boarders, is today a voluntary school which withdrew from the Free Scheme some years ago. Since then girls have been admitted and while they are not accepted as boarders, there exists the possibility that they may be. It has now been decided that both the Junior and Senior Houses of the college 'shall be governed by a Board of Governors' who will have over-all responsibility for deciding policy.

Provision is made on the Board of Governors for a strong lay presence but those chosen will inevitably be linked with the college either as members of the staff, parents, or ex-pupils. A somewhat unexpected clause of the Constitution is 12(a), which lays down the conditions in accordance with which a lay person may be appointed headmaster. This situation is likely to arise only in the event of a Dominican not being proposed for the post. And, as though to guard against such a happening, the Provincial of the Order has the right to veto any appointment 'on grounds of faith and morals only'.

A clause which proposes to introduce 'Visitations' may meet with less than warm enthusiasm. This allows a member of the Board of Governors to undertake an official visit to the college and to report on the visit in writing. Advance notice has, however, to be given, the agreement of the class teacher sought and a copy of the report made available to him or her.

While the Order of St Dominic would appear to be facing squarely the demands of the twentieth century, what the future holds for boarding schools and for Church schools in general remains uncertain. The monastic-type of school always tended towards exclusiveness. The extent to which such schools developed in Ireland owes much to the authority exercised in education by the Church, but the future is likely to see a lessening of such authority. Teacher representation on all educational boards is now guaranteed by the State nor is it likely that parents will recognize the validity of any custodians of culture in whose election they have no say.

Self-management of schools may follow from the gradual increase in lay control but with governments prepared to devolve authority on local bodies, it is a not unlikely development. It would then be for the local body to provide the school budget and for the headmaster to decide on the spending.

How the Newbridge experiment will work out, only time will tell. I would like to think that those who, in drawing up the new constitution for the college, have shown both imagination and courage, will now give thought to eliminating the private right to buy education. It is hardly consistent with the aims of a religious order to sustain privilege and maintain the divisions in our society which access to an expensive education serves but to perpetuate. The Dominican friars have taught generations to look on human life *sub specie aeternitatis*. May we not now look to them to make an effort, however small, to lessen privilege and, by doing so, offer us hope that we may yet have

> a country
> Where light equal, like the shine from snow,
> Strikes all faces.

NINE

St Paul's — Mountjoy / Mount Temple

HAVING ABSORBED WHAT I CONSIDERED sufficient of the Thomist philosophy, I 'exchanged' the Dominicans for the Vincentians and came to St Paul's College, Raheny, on the north side of Dublin, in 1956. For me it was a return to familiar ground. When teaching in Crumlin, part of my work entailed cycling across the city during my lunch hour to take afternoon classes in the Árd-Scoil which Mr Byrne also operated at the corner of Castle Avenue and Seafield Road. I had of course also taught for a brief period in Kostka College which was on Seafield Road.

Changing from the Newbridge college to one in Dublin was more than a geographical change. The Dominicans are an order of Preachers, the Vincentians have always had close links with the teaching profession. Their most famous teacher-training college in the English-speaking world is Strawberry Hill, near Twickenham in London, but they have also been in charge of St Patrick's College, Drumcondra, since 1875.

The difference in the approach of each order to the education of boys lay in the method adopted. The Dominicans reposed total confidence in the ability of each teacher and this, while welcome because of the freedom it allowed, did lead to a certain unevenness in what was done by individual teachers of the same subject. My headmaster at St Paul's, Father Moran, while not at all authoritarian, did lay down ground rules for the conduct of classes and he must have been among the first to encourage inter-disciplinary meetings between teachers of related subjects.

My three years in St Paul's also gave me an insight into the vital importance of the national schools. St Paul's was fortunate to have had some first-rate national schools 'feeding' boys from the age of twelve into the first year classes of its secondary school. In fact, one of the schools, Belgrove, used to provide almost the entire honours class each year. Yet St Paul's also had a preparatory department for pupils from the age of eight and of this I have nothing good to say. The teaching was usually indifferent, often downright poor, but parents did not seem to care once their offspring were assured entry to the secondary department. It had nothing to recommend it.

It is not always easy for a teacher to explain why one school attracts more than another. The curriculum in each is similar, the ability range of the pupils not very different, the salary scales alike. At St Paul's my teaching load was light as numbers were still low and I had but two pupils in my Leaving Certificate French class. Yet, when a vacancy for a teacher was advertised in Mountjoy School in 1960, I eagerly applied for it.

An odd incident then occurred. I had no contract of employment which was not a matter of surprise since, in my experience, religious orders did not always pay heed to Department regulations in that respect and, some might add, only rarely in many other respects. A craven Department of Education dared not insist. I had mentioned this absence of a contract to my headmaster as one of the reasons for my leaving. Two days later, *after* my appointment to Mountjoy School had been confirmed, he knocked at my classroom door and handed me a contract form. I kept it as a souvenir because in the course of fifty years' teaching, only once before had I been given one, and that was in Northern Ireland.

* * *

The Mountjoy School that I joined had not always been on the Malahide Road in north Dublin. A century earlier it had been at Santry, before in 1896 it moved to Mountjoy Square. To the half century spent in what was then one of the capital's most exclusive residential areas it owes the name by which it became known to generations of schoolboys. Once upon a time there were schools similar to Mountjoy belonging to the Incorporated Society for Promoting Protestant Schools in many parts of Ireland. Falling numbers had brought about closures and amalgamations.

Schools more than any other human institution tend to become known through their headmaster. In a period of almost seventy years Mountjoy had but two, The Reverend William Anderson (1896-1939) and Mr William Tate (1939-1964). Each left a lasting imprint on the school which long enjoyed a high reputation, especially for the quality of its mathematical teaching. There must still be hundreds of ex-pupils who remember with affection the great Maths teacher, 'Jackie' Campbell, who for fifty years simplified and solved for them the most abstruse problems.

Even those inquiry agents of another day, the inspectors of schools, were impressed when in 1910 three of them, Wright, Maguire and O'Neill, spent a few days on general inspection in Mountjoy Square. Commenting on the Senior Grade, O'Neill observed that the pupils did 'two rather difficult questions in Arithmetic for me in capital style'.

The terms of my own appointment did not include Games but I did have to take pupils on the Wednesday half-day to the 'Public Baths and Wash-house' in Tara Street. Dante makes no mention of such places in his *Inferno* but public baths at 4 p.m. on a day in early summer after some hundreds of children had immersed themselves in liquid chlorine was worthy of his attention. Falling fully-clothed into the pool, jumping from the overhead girders, and seeing how long smaller boys could be held under the water, were the most favoured activities of those whose safety was in my hands. A day in a dark room and the application of cold compresses generally saw me fully restored.

I made little effort to conceal my relief when the headmaster suggested that I might like to take evening duty in the school at weekends and leave Swimming Duty to a new junior master. Weekend duty was never excessively onerous and in the summer term all those boys who were members of the Scout Troop went to camp. On such occasions it was the duty of the master-on-duty to issue 'leave-outs'. One Friday a boy named Thorpe came to me for the customary permission and the following dialogue (or something very similar) ensued:

'Please, sir, may I have week-end leave to go camping?'

'Certainly' I replied. 'A splendid idea. Good bracing exercise. Are you all hiking to the hills?'

'No, sir, we have a special bus.'

'Ah, well, and when you get there you will gather

firewood, rub some sticks together and get the fire going.'

'No, sir, there is a Perma-glow stove in the scout hut.'

'I see. Well, what then? Snare a rabbit and cook it?'

'No, sir, matron has given us pre-packed meals.'

'Ah, splendid. Then you will all sit around the campfire and sing rousing songs.'

'No, sir. We have tickets for the disco in the Community Hall.'

'Well, after all that you will be well ready for a sleep on a bed of moss and bracken, beneath the stars.'

'No, sir. We all have sleeping bags with a thermostat which controls the temperature throughout the night.'

The foregoing illustrates if it does nothing else, the truth of the saying 'Ask a silly question and you get a silly answer'.

I found standards of work, especially among the seniors, very high. This may in part have been due to the inflow of boys aged sixteen or seventeen from Kilkenny, Sligo and Multyfarnham who came to the 'Joy in order to complete their secondary education. Nor did the close links which had always existed between the school and Northern Ireland end with the Treaty. For some years afterwards a number of boys entered the examination for clerkships in the Northern Civil Service. In his book entitled *Working at Stormont*, John A. Oliver mentions many of them by name: 'R. F. R. Dunbar, G. W. Nixon, R. R. Butler, L. C. Dennis, W. J. Arthurs, A. H. Henderson, J. S. H. Gaw – about three or four each year out of a total of ten to twenty entrants a year, a truly remarkable state of affairs and a tribute to the enterprise of the Mountjoy Staff.'

That staff remained remarkably unchanged and when in 1960 I went there, I found that Campbell, Sutton, Webb,

Simmons, Le Blanc and Hughes had each completed over thirty years in the service of the school. The headmasters who followed Tate were faced with changes not altogether due to the passage of time. Under Brooks (1965-1977), a merger was effected between Mountjoy School and the Hibernian Marine School in nearby Clontarf, and a year later the Bertrand and Rutland High School in Eccles Street joined the educational consortium.

These endings and new beginnings paved the way for the comprehensive school which took the name of Mount Temple. This recalls a farm of that name where the school now stands and which was owned by the Colley family, maternal grand-parents of Elizabeth Bowen. It is of interest that in an interview published twenty years before the present school was formally opened, Mr Tate was quoted as saying:

> I think it quite definite that if, supposing the Protestant Churches got together and went to the Minister and said, 'We would like a comprehensive school in such and such a place for our people', provided they were satisfied that there was a need for it, I do not imagine there would be any difficulty in establishing a school with Protestant representation on the same basis as comprehensive schools now being built with Roman Catholic representation.

The headmaster who guided the school through all the changes necessitated by two amalgamations, the decision to go co-educational and the re-opening of the old school as a modern comprehensive, was John Brooks. If Tate was a headmaster in line of descent from such a man as Arnold of

Rugby, Brooks was the twentieth century academic concerned for the rights of a profession charged with what he would consider that most important of tasks, education. He was forthright in making what he considered to be legitimate demands on the State and persuasive and tenacious in presenting his case. He deplored any distinction between Catholic and Protestant in matters strictly secular, and criticized the government for making such a distinction.

John Medlycott (1977-), who followed Brooks, is a pragmatist who from the outset showed himself resilient and resourceful. With a pupil population of six hundred and fifty, far wider in its social and religious range from that known to his predecessor, he has pushed aside any unnecessary tyrannies of dress and custom and has concentrated on the development of what is rich and worthwhile in each student.

Before leaving the staff on whom the reputation of any school rests, I do not think that there are many old Mountjoy boys who would easily answer the following questions. What teacher edited *An Phoblacht*, fought in the Spanish Civil War, became a major in the International Brigade and was sentenced to death? The answer is Frank Ryan who, while doing a degree in Celtic Studies at UCD, taught Irish for a brief period to the senior classes.

Mountjoy School, when I came to know it, had many observances and customs preserved probably from the days in Santry. *Exeats* were granted by the master on duty only after a scrutiny to ensure that any junior boys seeking 'leave out' were wearing school caps. Morning Assembly was always taken by the headmaster with two other masters in attendance. Mid-morning slices of bread and butter were called 'dodges', a word which I found also existed in

Kilkenny College.

The big events of the school year were Prize Day and Sports Day. Prize Day followed an unchanging ritual which began after lunch as the first cars came up the gravel drive to be parked at the direction of the school sergeant or Tom Roche. In the teachers' Common Room gowns purchased in the long ago, and now little more than moth-ravaged strips of cloth, were being matched with brightly coloured academic hoods hired for the occasion.

Punctually at five minutes to three the headmaster put his head in and called out 'Come along, gentlemen', and the *cortège* of masters set off down the corridor towards the gloomy and architecturally appalling Assembly Hall. Only a mace-bearer was lacking!

It was a moving occasion for those who recalled other such days when as pupils they had trotted up to receive their prize and enjoy a moment of glory as they were congratulated by the Archbishop of Dublin before returning with a volume or volumes from the APCK Bookshop. As the winter day darkened outside and balcony lights were turned on, all listened once more to the words 'and now let us stand for the closing hymn and remain standing for the benediction'.

There are changeless moments in the life of a teacher unknown to those in other professions. He takes farewell each summer of those talents he has helped to develop and he welcomes each autumn newcomers of whose aptitudes and talents he knows nothing. Like most boarding schools, Mountjoy had always a number of boys whose fathers and even grandfathers had sat in the same classrooms if not at the same desks. This gave to life within the walls a warmth and intimacy which I felt each morning as I turned the handle of the outer door to be greeted by a combination of smells –

floor-polish, cabbage and embrocation. Terms followed one another with the unchanging rhythm of the seasons. Muddied blue and black jerseys in the changing room signalled the onset of winter, to be followed by the appearance of flannels as the spring sunshine dissolved the last of the May frosts. Summer with the heavy Atco lawnmower weaving patterns of alternating light and dark green on the cricket pitch while a group of 'conscripts' in the charge of a prefect gave a coat of paint to the pavilion.

Odd as it may seem, it was at a time when I was totally happy in my teaching and convinced that Mountjoy School or, as it had just become, Mount Temple Comprehensive, would be my last school, that I left.

Admittedly I had preferred it as Mountjoy. I believed very strongly in the tradition of solid endeavour that Mountjoy seemed to represent. The curriculum may have been limited, the school itself antiquated, but for those within it – boarders as well as day boys – it represented security, companionship and an education that laid a foundation for future study.

Then it became Mount Temple. Boarders disappeared. Girls appeared. Cricket disappeared. Trampoline appeared. The Nissen hut disappeared. A gymnasium and, later, a concert hall appeared. I came to like what appeared, including a room for my subject, French, and even if my teaching of that subject owed little to the language laboratory and much to my insistence that knowledge of the *passé composé* rivalled the observance of the Ten Commandments in importance, my pupils and I, so I like to think, got on well together.*

---

*To mention some ex-pupils of Mount Temple and not others seems hard to justify but if I confine myself to those who have achieved worldwide

It was then 1977 and I had for some years been on the Irish Committee of the United World Colleges. An effort to get Departmental sanction for the secondment of a teacher to one of these colleges was unsuccessful. It then occurred to me that I might go. I applied to the Canadian college, the Lester B. Pearson College of the Pacific, and by Easter of that year a letter of acceptance reached me.

To write of the college in Canada is work for another day. The island of Vancouver on which it is situated is both scenically and climatically the most delightful part of British Columbia of which Stephen Leacock said that had he known it was so beautiful, he would have been born there. I return there with a feeling of affection that previously I had reserved for Cork. Had I gone there as a young man, 'O Canada' might well have displaced 'The Boys from Fairhill' as my favourite song.

---

acclaim, I may escape criticism. Paul Hewson (1972-78), Richard Evans (1973-78), Larry Mullen (1974-76) and Adam Clayton (1976-78) have remained together since their schooldays to form U-2.

TEN

Valediction

WE ALL OF US have our favourite quotations and I propose to begin what may be called a valedictory chapter with mine: 'It is possible that the proper time to attend school is when one has retired on pension and can afford the time.'

I am now 'retired on pension' and it is very pleasant to go back even occasionally, meet former colleagues and recall long-dead teachers with whom we worked and whose eccentricities we remember. No one, no matter how lunatic his or her behaviour, can measure up to the teacher whom the Endowed School Commissioners encountered in Ballyroan, County Laois (then Queen's County) in 1881. Of him they reported in a memorable passage:

> He holds his place by appointment of the patron, and is not removable by the headmaster or the Commissioners, or perhaps by anyone. The present usher is a man of above eighty or ninety years of age, indeed he may possibly be one hundred; he is so dull and shrivelled with age that he only comes in late, and is unable to teach anything; I do not think he comprehended who I was or what I wanted. His appointment dates from the remote

> past and when I asked what his qualifications were, or had once been, I could learn nothing but some vague legends about his great severity in early youth, in fact I was told that he once pult (*sic*) the ear off a boy.

Surely he was the original of the 'aged, aged man' of whom the White Knight in *Alice in Wonderland* asks, 'How is it that you live?'

The teachers who are most easily remembered are often those who were so blazingly mad that stories and legends of them abound and are magnified with each telling. One teacher with whom I taught read the Adventures of Gussie Goose, serialized in the *Irish Independent*, to his senior classes every morning and, the effort proving too much for him, then retired to the staff room and put his feet up. He was a gentle, peace-loving man and only once did I see him explode into such a state of wrath as might have made the Ayatollah tremble. That was when at an Examiners' Conference on the Intermediate Latin paper, much time was given to deciding whether to give five marks or eight marks to candidates who were able to state correctly that Vercingetorix was a Gaulish chieftain.

Eccentric characters now seem fewer, possibly because of the more professional approach to the job and the insistence by school principals that qualifications must meet job requirements. What on earth was required of those who, in my own lifetime, answered the following advertisements?

> S.T. Required September, School South of Ireland; major subjects Irish, English, Geography and Drawing (through Irish), History; other subjects: Maths, Latin, French, Commerce, Singing, also supervise games, state

qualifications, experience, results; also lowest salary required. Box 13428.

Irish Independent, 16 March 1944.

Wanted, Secondary Teacher. Honours M.A., subjects, Irish English, Latin, Greek, French, Maths to Leaving Certificate. History, Geography, Drawing, Science to Intermediate: salary £180, outdoor. Box T 1983.

The Irish Times, 3 February 1953.

Teacher for school in Midlands, January 1975. Subjects: English, Irish, Mathematics, Science to Leaving Certificate. Geography, History, Drawing, Latin to Intermediate Certificate. Help with games an advantage. Box A8297.

The Irish Press, 22 November 1974.

Pay in earlier days was often uncertain and long before educational theorists sought to make 'work experience' an essential component of any teacher education course, teachers were known 'to make a book' at Fairyhouse Races on Easter Monday and operate the three-card trick at the Ballyboy (Dunmanway) point-to-point.

Such expedients are no longer necessary largely because of the growth in the number of teachers, particularly lay, and the strength of the teacher unions. There are today 10,018 lay secondary school teachers and slightly over 2000 religious teaching in secondary schools. Anyone seeking examples of discrimination on the basis of sex may find material for debate in two further statistics: 4 per cent of principals in Vocational schools are women, and 5 per cent in Community and Comprehensive schools!

The future must see changes in each of these sets of

figures. It is unlikely that the number of religious in teaching will increase, and it is likely that the number of women principals will increase. Principals may be given a different role which will see them involved more in policy-making, while staff, with the co-operation of parents, will deal with administrative issues. This will become possible as new learning systems are developed and 'schooling' no longer takes place only within a school building. Information technology will be developed to the point that pupils will do much of their learning at home.

Any change from the centralizing tyrannies of the box-like, compartmentalized schoolroom and the teaching of single subjects for set amounts of time will give a new freedom for use in new ways. Leisure will no longer be something for after-school or after-work, it will be an 'activity' to be prepared for and enjoyed. This sharing of life and leisure with others may help to lessen the high level of distrust between different social groupings and make for better worker-management relationship.

This is one aspect of education to which the new local education councils will have to give early attention. The subject-based curriculum is doomed and team-teaching, multi-disciplinary work will prepare the way for the gradual dismantling of the examination system. The world outside the school no longer has the same need for those neat, supervised examinations in which marks are given to those who can best compress their knowledge into precise answers in a precise period of time. It is, I think, not difficult to sustain the thesis that examinations, buttressed by the schools, ensure that there is little social mobility in Irish life. Children of professional workers move into the professional field. Children of manual workers, especially those who are unskilled or semi-skilled, seldom do so.

It is time that the pro-examination culture which has developed in Ireland as elsewhere should now be challenged. What hope is there of developing flexibility in their later studies and of altering the rigid class structure of our society if we hypnotize children into believing that examinations are what education is all about?

Schools place insufficient emphasis on children applying what they learn. Practical capability, the skills needed to design things, should be part of the curriculum for all children. For non-academic children to follow academic courses with mediocre results can be permanently harmful and success as a craft-worker, artist or professional footballer should be considered as appropriate for a school-leaver as going to university or entering the bank. Where is the possibility of developing a spirit of lasting co-operation between different elements in our society when pupils are streamed into clever and not-so-clever groups; among the clever there is competition, and among the not-so-clever there is apathy, indifference and a sense of failure.

I have seen the breakdown, physical as well as emotional, of too many who left school with honours in their subjects but with their creative abilities undeveloped and with little self-confidence and no sense of self worth.

George Bernard Shaw claimed that the National Gallery of Ireland played a priceless part in his education and, in his will, he ensured that for fifty years after his death the Gallery would receive one third of the royalties derived from his published works. We do provide better opportunities than ever before for more young people to pass examinations but we do not always give sufficient thought to the creative instincts within each of them. It would be sad if, while spreading widely the range of education, especially at second and third-level, we remained hostile rather than hospitable to creativeness in the arts. An education system which does not take sufficient account of art and music and drama is not just deficient in the opportunities for expression but also in the opportunities for knowledge it gives to young people.

The existence of single-sex schools did, in its own way, contribute to this indifference to the arts and any attempt to interest pupils in the arts was largely confined to girls' schools. I never could see how any argument justified segregation on the basis of sex, yet many schools controlled by religious continue to maintain the division which, of course, ends in any case at the school gates. Even were there no pedagogical reasons for educating boys and girls together, there are strong financial and professional reasons for doing so. Building costs are thereby reduced, administrative costs are less, while teachers as a professional class are free to offer their services to the community without distinction of sex.

There would have been less need to maintain single-sex schools if the Catholic Church had given spiritual guidance to *all* the school-going population under its control. The Church, however, chose to ignore those pupils who attended vocational schools until such time as instruction in Religious Education was paid for by the Vocational Education Committees.

Even in the field of sport the division between 'them' and 'us' was absolute, and I cannot recall any sporting fixture taking place between a secondary school in which I taught and a vocational school. This meant that to such existing divisions in schools as sex and sect there was added sport.

I never did work up any enthusiasm for school games.

I knew them to be used to discriminate between those who could kick a ball and those who could not. Those who could and got on the first fifteen enjoyed certain concessions; they might sleep in and miss morning Mass if they were so minded, they got milk and biscuits or bovril at the morning break and porridge at night. If all that was not enough to arouse rebellious feelings among those who would never make even the tenth fifteen, there were Victory buns if they won. But, *vae victis*, no buns if they lost! So was the sporting spirit engendered in schools I have known and in some of which I have taught.

It makes me feel that Orwell's views on football were close to my own:

> I loathed the game, and since I see no pleasure or usefulness in it, it was very difficult for me to show courage at it. Football, it seemed to me, is not really played for the pleasure of kicking a ball about, but is a species of fighting. The lovers of football are large, boisterous, nobbly boys who are good at knocking down and trampling on slightly smaller boys. That was the pattern of school life – a continuous triumph of the strong over the weak. Virtue consisted in winning!*

If the game of rugby appears to draw most of my criticism, it is because of the reverent seriousness with which the game is treated in certain boarding schools. Is it not a sign of the immaturity of those in charge of the education of boys to drive rigorously and relentlessly the school fifteen from

*'Such, Such Were the Joys' in *The Collected Essays, Journalism and Letters of George Orwell*, Vol. 4, p.411.

October onwards while ignoring the many for whom rugby and, indeed, all team games are no more than aimless activities? Much of the hysteria tolerated if not encouraged by the school authorities when cup-tie time comes round, and much of the emotive language used in pre-match talks, would seem to confirm this view.

Fanaticism takes on a somewhat different form when one considers the place of hurling and Gaelic football in the schools. In most educational systems, and not just in Ireland, there is an instinct to preserve what is considered to be of cultural value. This particular value is often hard to define. It may be the native language, it may be traditional music, it may be some time-honoured pastime. In Ireland this instinct has operated with unusual strength, perhaps because of the feeling of encirclement, in favour of the games of hurling and Gaelic football. 'The games of the Empire', as rugby and soccer have been called, were banned in many schools and what would be described as 'a preservation order' placed on hurling and football.

I have a clear memory of one Prize Day when the headmaster spoke for twenty minutes, during which he dilated on the achievements of the rugby team without once mentioning the academic achievement of a school-leaver who had been awarded first place in a University Entrance Scholarship examination of that year. It all seemed a world away from the ideal of an education based on the mind and the spirit of man. But it was applauded and the parents departed seemingly satisfied that 'the foolish propulsion of solid globes through the air' was not without advantage for their offspring.

Many schools which have laid out magnificent playing fields have singularly failed to encourage the planting of trees, shrubs and flowers. I do not think it unreasonable to expect schools to make some effort to improve their external surroundings and also make their interiors less bleak and cheerless. I have visited almost one hundred second-level schools during the past six years while supervising student teachers for the Higher Diploma at Trinity College. Not a single shrub or tree is to be seen on the expanse of grassland leading to some of these schools and not an original painting or good reproduction on the walls of corridor or classroom.

AE spoke truth when he said that a nation can now become cultivated 'only in so far as the average man, not the exceptional person, is cultivated and has knowledge of the thought, imagination and intellectual history of his nation. Where there is a general culture its effects are seen in the houses, the pictures, the home and garden, and the arts of life: a better taste is manifest. Almost insensibly beauty enters the household and what is meant by a civilisation at last becomes apparent'.

Teachers have been likened to men leaning on a bridge and watching the water eddying and flowing beneath them. They see it as an image of school and of the pupils who each year leave. Some are swept on to success, others drift into backwater currents, others still founder and are lost to view. It is a profession which, because of an urge to look backwards, has its moments of loneliness:

Uaigneach céird an oide
Mar mháithrín léi féin,
Taréis imeacht a cloinne
*Thar táirsigh i gcéin.**

---

*Ceann an Bhóthair ag Séamus Ó hAodha, M.A., Brún agus Ó Nuallain Teo. 1966.

Appendix A

SIX PIONEERING EDUCATIONISTS

WHY SIX? Why not include all those who have lent shape and purpose to the Irish system of education over the past fifty years? No process of selection can ever be entirely satisfactory. There will always be omissions, but perhaps someone someday will compile a Biographical Dictionary of Irish Educationists. Meanwhile, I have chosen those whom I have known and who, I believe, provoked discussion, developed policies, challenged accepted theories and, at times, disturbed complacency.

Education programmes wither and grow stale but there is much that is enduring, much that is permanent in the work of these six men. The beliefs each one held, the convictions that inspired them, the attitudes they adopted, the tensions they caused may now be forgotten, but the education given in our schools and colleges today is part of their legacy.

It is not generally realized that for long – certainly since 1878 – many of our educational ideas came to us second-hand from England. This is not criticism of the ideas themselves. Rather it is an admission that we in Ireland were satisfied to live in the shadow of the English system. When Patrick Cannon (see below) first drew attention to certain defects in this inherited system he was attacked for doing so. Yet all he did was to point to the resources of the nation, the need to use them fully and, at the same time, stimulate the social imagination to use them equitably.

There are no themes common to these educationists. Each exercised independent judgment on the problems confronting him. They were not crusaders nor did they organize pressure groups to promote their views, but their impact was the dynamic that made advance possible.

PATRICK F. CANNON

b. Donegal town, 1908. d. 1968
School: St Eunan's, Letterkenny
University: University College, Dublin
Called to the Bar, 1924

Anyone teaching as I was during the 'thirties must have been tranquillized by the quiet that prevailed on all things great and small in the world of education. Not that the Department of Education was inactive. Conscientiously and painstakingly, it marshalled facts and figures which it published many years later when any interest or controversy these might have aroused had been stilled by the passage of time.

The first stir, 'ripple' might be more apt, on the placid surface of education may be said to have been seen in 1947 when Patrick Cannon, barrister as well as teacher, opened a co-educational lay school in the Dublin suburb of Sandymount. There was not an event of any great importance, certainly no mention of it appears in the national newspapers of the day. Yet some years later,* Cannon was to be referred to in Dáil Éireann by the Minister for Education, Dr Hillery, as 'that man' and a document, which was largely his work, became the subject of a day-long debate.

The minister had refused to grant recognition as a negotiating body to the Federation of Irish Secondary Schools, founded in Cork in 1945 by Seán Ó hUrmholtaigh, and embracing some fifty schools owned and staffed by lay teachers. He based his refusal on the misleading nature of

---

*13 December 1962.

Patrick F. Cannon

the title which he said purported to be that of a body representative of Irish secondary schools when, in fact, it represented no more than 'about one-tenth of our secondary schools'. Cannon pointed out that such a title was no more misleading than that of 'The Schoolmasters' Association' or 'The Catholic Headmasters' Association'. The Minister defended the recognition given to these by saying that their titles too would be misleading 'but for their long period of existence'.

The Federation may not have had a 'long period of existence' but it was, nevertheless, heir to a valued tradition. When the hedge schools of Ireland came to be replaced by schools largely in the control of religious bodies, the independence of mind and character which had always marked the layman as teacher was lost. The Federation of Catholic Lay Secondary Schools, as it later came to be called, came into existence because of the need to express attitudes to education which none of the larger bodies fully represented, and to provide education in areas where larger communities would have found it difficult to survive.

They built without loans, without grants, without the blessing of Church or the benefits of State. Despite the uncertainties, the difficulties, the disappointments, they managed to keep fees low and standards high. The names of those founder members deserve to be remembered. They were: S. Hamilton (Bandon), P. Cannon (Sandymount), V. Russell and T. McGrath (Cahir), S. Donnelly (Glasheen), P. O Ceileachair (Buttevant), D. Dilworth (Dunmanway), T. Kerrisk (Castleisland), G. Dineen (Clonakilty), T. O Maoilean (Tyrellspass), J. O'Dwyer (Killorglin), Mrs J. Savage (Drumcollogher), Mrs J. Breen (Newcastlewest).

Cannon was the driving force behind much of the work

undertaken by the Federation. He it was who first drew attention to the imbalance in educational provision in the Republic, to the need for a far wider spread of post-primary education if the country was to fulfil the hopes not only of visionaries but of economists. He it was who drew attention to the almost complete absence of facilities for pupils in secondary schools to develop an appreciation of design and craftsmanship in wood and metal. What he said in the course of an interview given to *The Irish Times* in 1963 is as relevant today as it was then: 'I do not believe that the education of any boy can be described as complete and rounded-off unless he has been trained in the oldest skill known to mankind, the ability to use his hands.'

In that same interview he quoted from the prospectus of Manchester Grammar, then as now one of the most distinguished schools in Britain:

> The Handcraft Department offers facilities to boys to develop an appreciation of design and craftsmanship in wood and metal. After a basic course in the theory and practice of the crafts, boys may continue this kind of work both during timetable periods and each evening. The drawing office, the woodwork and machine shops, the forge and foundry are available for boys to continue their craft whenever they are free, enabling them to pursue their interests to the full extent of their individual capabilities.

If the Minister for Education had been irritated by the pretensions of the Federation to represent the lay teacher, he must have resented even more the Federation's *Investment in Education in the Republic of Ireland* (1962). This document anticipated the more profound study in 1965 by the OECD team under the Chairmanship of Professor Patrick Lynch of University College, Dublin, which Akenson describes as 'the first governmental document to treat education as a social and economic activity and not chiefly as a theological abstraction or a linguistic exercise'.

If someone were to ask how Cannon came to achieve so much, the answer could readily be given by saying that he was resourceful, far-seeing, hardworking and, in a sense, indifferent to the prestige with which institutions and individuals, too, like to clothe themselves. He had positive ideals, he put them into practice in the school he founded, and he prepared to spread them through the members of the Federation. He was among the first to advocate Special Allowances for headmasters and assistant headmasters, recognition of teaching service abroad, oral tests in all language examinations, posts of Special Responsibility and posts as Heads of Department. There is nothing particularly innovative about such recommendations today but in the Ireland of 1960 they were seen as almost revolutionary.

His own school, Sandymount High, is the finest monument to his work. In opening it he was, he said, perpetuating one of the oldest traditions in Irish education. He quoted the words of Cardinal Newman and echoed his belief that 'To open the mind, to correct it, to refine it, to enable it to know, and to digest, master, rule and use its knowledge, to give it power over its own faculties, application, flexibilities, method, critical exactness, sagacity, resource, address, eloquent expression is the aim of a truly liberal education.' These precepts informed his teaching and have continued to influence the work of the school under his son, Conall, who took over on his father's death in 1968.

THE REVEREND DONAL CREGAN, C.M.

b. Newcastlewest, County Limerick, 1911
School: Castleknock College
University: University College, Dublin
Graduated in History, 1933
Chairman, Irish Manuscripts Commission

The national teacher has been a figure of varying importance in the social life of the country for more than one hundred and fifty years. In rural Ireland he ranks with the priest and doctor. In urban Ireland his status is less clearly defined and only in recent years has he emerged as a professional figure of substance.

Public attitudes towards him were often ambiguous; he was respected for his learning, but in a country where lay leadership was not encouraged he was seen as subservient to his manager, the local priest or rector.

Preparation for a teaching life that extended over forty-five years was conducted in an atmosphere little different from that of a boarding school and subject to many of the same irksome restrictions. It was monastic in its insistence on the observance of times for rising and sleeping, for meals and leisure. The curriculum was limited and the arts largely ignored.

Change came from a somewhat unexpected source. The Vincentian Order who had control of the largest training college in the country, St Patrick's, Drumcondra, had also an impressive boarding school on the outskirts of Dublin. Its president in 1957, when he was appointed to take charge of St Patrick's, was Father Cregan. He would be pardoned if, on hearing the news, he showed some dismay.

The building was drab, the two-year course uninspiring and the opportunities for those entering on a career in primary teaching limited. However, the moment for change and the man to effect it had converged. Father Cregan's own teaching experience as well as his strength of character gave him a stability of base from which to innovate so that when he proposed the four-year degree course for teachers, he did not have to raise his voice. He was listened to. Neither assertive nor aggressive, he had analysed trends and arrived at what was to prove the correct decision.

By the time, some twenty years later, that he left St Patrick's, the teachers had a magnificent new college, a college that had expanded from an enrolment of two hundred male students to one of nine hundred male and female students. A full degree course had been devised, a research centre created, a department for teachers dealing with special problems established and a *Journal of Education* launched.

The Educational Research Unit was, I feel, a development particularly dear to him and he never failed to insist that only in an atmosphere free from political and public pressures could it prosper. He was equally insistent that research should not be insensitive to the needs of society 'outside the walls' of the college. His model would be the medieval universities with their passionate espousal of all sorts of causes and their often turbulent relationship with the world around them.

It is hard to imagine a revolution, for it was little else, taking place so unobtrusively. Courses, curriculum, content, each came under his scrutiny. He was never afraid to stimulate doubt, if it was at all constructive, ever prepared to oppose indifference which he saw as destructive. Answer-

The Reverend Donal Cregan

ing a question, he once remarked that all too rarely are students asked to think for themselves, to judge for themselves, to make decisions for themselves and, as he added, 'that is what education is all about'. The positions occupied today by many of those who studied under him point to his encouragement of what may be called intellectual adventuring.

Builders, architects, landscape artists, as well as students and staff, had their problems solved by this quiet-spoken man who, when all was completed, returned gratefully to the study of legal aspects of the Stuart administration in Ireland.

Despite the many calls on his time, nothing ever appeared too unimportant or too irrelevant when it concerned the assumptions, aims or methods of advancing the cause of education. Nor did he emphasize the distinction between laity and religious, believing that in education each must neither ask for privileges nor be denied equality. As far back as 1957 he spoke of the need for more scope for the ambition and initiative of the laity: 'I would', he said, 'envisage nuns, priests and brothers teaching school under lay control.' He appeared to be able to assess in advance the human consequences of proposed changes and, while he was one of the first to welcome the intervention of the State in education, he made clear that increased government support should mean greater, not less, freedom for the teacher.

Of few educationists can it be said that they influenced education at all levels. Father Cregan was, in turn, headmaster of a secondary school, president of a primary teachers' training college and, briefly, at his request, Professor of Education. These interests were known to the public. Far less was known of the range and depth of scholarship which brought him recognition from, among others, the Gulbenkian Foundation, UNESCO and the Comparative Education Society in Europe.

Unobtrusive and self-effacing, he would have been equally at home in a sixteenth-century Italian court or, a century later, in a Hapsburg palace. Fortune decreed otherwise. Today, as Chairman of the Irish Manuscripts Commission, he surveys the background to the many events which in the course of centuries shaped the lives and determined the destiny of our people.

DONOGH O'MALLEY

b. Limerick, 1921. d. 1968
Schools: Crescent College & Clongowes Wood College
University: University College, Galway
Graduated in Engineering, 1942

The country had to wait almost half a century before a Minister for Education came into office with the vision of changes needed, particularly in the secondary sector, and the courage to make the necessary changes. Nerve, even more than plain courage, and a considerable political majority were two requisites for confronting the Catholic Church in the area of secondary education. Few governments since 1921 had the political margin, none had the nerve.

When in July 1966 Donogh O'Malley was made Minister for Education, few eyebrows were raised. The general verdict was that it was not a very dramatic decision and that the former Minister for Health would soon learn that Ministers for Education might reign but not rule. Yet a mere four months later he announced in Dáil Éireann the introduction of a scheme proposing 'a supplementary State grant to schools in certain fee ranges on conditions that they will discontinue charging school fees, that is, that they will offer free education to all pupils'.

All O'Malley really did was to break through the barrier which had long given the fee-paying secondary schools the independence of the State they so prized. This he did by making full use of the word 'free'. Once parents got the drift of what it meant, enrolments at second-level schools increased at a rate embarrassing both to schools and

Donogh O'Malley

staffs forced to cope with pupils of a wider range of ability and social background in crowded classrooms.

What is not generally known is that the original scheme was intended to be implemented by drawing in only those schools generally run by communities of religious of which the Irish Christian Brothers and the Sisters of Mercy were the most prominent, charging very low fees.* O'Malley intended that the State should pay for each enrolled pupil in these schools the amount of the standard fee. These schools, in which most of the nation's children received their second-level education, could then expand and take in children whose parents could not afford *any* fees. The Archbishop of Dublin, John Charles McQuaid, sensing danger, instructed all schools to join the scheme. This had the effect of ending O'Malley's hope of supporting the underprivileged and leaving the well-to-do to pay for themselves. Many of the relatively high-charging schools further undermined the effectiveness of the scheme by charging 'extras', despite the warnings of the Department, for fringe activities such as art, music and games.

Within months the Department could publish a résumé of the scheme, from which it may be seen how eagerly it had been adopted:

SCHEME FOR THE PROVISION OF
FREE POST-PRIMARY EDUCATION

1. Of the nearly 600 secondary schools (over 100,000 pupils), those which agree to make no tuition charge will receive a grant of £25 per annum per pupil from the State.

All the secondary schools outside Dublin except five

*Often as low as £12 and rarely exceeding £25.

have opted for the new scheme.

Of the 102 secondary schools in Dublin 78 have joined.

This means that 97% of the secondary school children outside Dublin and 85% of those in Dublin receive free education. The free scheme applies right up to Leaving Certificate. The scheme applies only to day-pupils who form 78% of the whole.

2. All the 300 or so vocational schools (35,000 full-time pupils) are free of charge.

3. Fees may be charged to individual pupils for such subjects (e.g. instrumental music, ballet) as are taught to individual pupils, but not to the entire school. For a school's admission to the scheme, any subject which is on the school's general curriculum may not be charged for.

4. For the 42 Protestant schools a special scheme has had to be devised because the Protestant population is scattered.

The scheme gives the Protestant authorities an annual lump sum calculated on the basis of the total provided for the Catholic pupils. It is for the Protestant authorities to allocate this sum among Protestant pupils as they think fit in accordance with individual pupils' needs.

Today it is estimated that less than 8 per cent of the entire secondary school population attend fee-paying schools. The following figures will give an idea of the fees charged and the numbers on the rolls:

	Boarders	Day	Day	Boarders
Sligo Grammar School	135	205	£ 600	£1890
Newbridge College	150	280	£ 650	£2485
Newtown School	116	164	£1170	£2700
Ashton School	77	414	—	£1482
Kilkenny College	330	80	£ 700	£2100
Glenstal	179	—	—	£2985
Wilson's Hospital School	224	47	£ 555	£1420
Clongowes Wood College	380	—	—	£3000
King's Hospital School	368	230	£1314	£2919
Drogheda Grammar School	160	60	£ 230	£ 630
Blackrock College	200	700	£ 850	£2850
College of St Columba	250	60	£2400	£4080
St Andrew's College	60	650	£ 750	£ 850

Second-level enrolments rose rapidly from 148,000 in 1966/67 to 329,400 in 1984/85.

Why had the Republic to wait so long for a man prepared to rule as well as reign? Part of the reason lies in the dichotomous simplicity of the pro- and anti-Treaty parties, which was disastrous for an abstract subject like education. No Minister for Education wanted to rock the boat when, by maintaining its equilibrium and without altering the speed, he could appear to be guiding it towards nationally and, not less important, religiously desirable aims.

The work of O'Malley has often been classed as 'expansionist' in that he was chiefly interested in extending the spread of education. To accept such a limit to his work is to completely underrate the man. He saw everyone who mattered in education, received scores of deputations, listened with courteous attention to students in their 'teens as well as to bishops, showed heroic powers of endurance in sitting through seminars, conferences, lectures, teach-ins, etc. Urbane discussion and savage debate were equally to his liking but no one dared risk wasting his time on frivolous aspects of serious themes – the sudden drop in temperature chilled bones whether clothed in black or otherwise.

Ireland had need of him to erase the religious differences that had for long bedevilled all educational discussion in the Republic. To him the words 'clergy and laity', 'Protestant and Catholic', 'National and Trinity', were politically irrelevant. He may not have indulged in daydreams, he may have shown impatience with those who did, but he had a remorseless clarity of vision that gave shape and substance to his work.

He was criticized for acting too hurriedly, for failure to consult the myriad educational organizations, for making decisions before ensuring that he had the resources to implement them. But for anyone dissatisfied, as he was, with the tortoise pace of educational advance, he did the only thing possible. He prepared a plan, he made a pronouncement and he proceeded on his way. That he seemed to ignore legitimate objections to his plans failed somehow to shock the people who grasped, even imperfectly, that they were witnesses to a sociological revolution. And it may be sociologists rather than educationists who will one day evaluate the measure of his achievement.

H. R. CATHCART

b. Dublin, 1926
School: St Patrick's Cathedral School
University: Trinity College, Dublin
Graduated in Modern History & Political Science, 1951

There were few forthright, well-informed commentators on the educational system during the long complacent years before and after the Second World War. The inevitability of stern clerical opposition to change, the unwillingness of a government department, caparisoned in its safety jacket of inactivity, to attempt anything but the most modest of structural alterations in the system seemed to have stifled comment, killed criticism.

To this acceptance of mediocrity Hector Rex Cathcart, headmaster of the Royal School, Raphoe, and later of Sandford Park School in Dublin, was an exception. Himself a graduate in modern history and political science, he had a Janus-like perspective of the educational scene. As a historian he could look backwards at the monolithic structure based firmly on a religious foundation which the British government had helped to build in 1831 and to which an extra dimension had been added in 1878. As a student of political science he was aware of the restless energies waiting to be released through a system of education whose object would no longer be 'the preservation of privilege' (the words are Cathcart's) but rather the development of talent wherever it lay.

While his ideas on education were still but taking shape and when his teaching load was well in excess of twenty hours a week, he opened up dialogue between Protestant

H. R. Cathcart

and Catholic in the course of a Prize Day speech in 1960 as headmaster of Raphoe Royal School in County Donegal. As always he was eager to promote constructive ways of uniting the different elements in Irish life with their varying traditions and cultures.

His speech focused attention on the vital importance of education, a subject to which he was to return in many articles and broadcasts in the years that followed. Long before the comprehensive ideal in education became a practical reality, he had expressed the hope that in its full sense it could be the salvation of our island:

> Therein lies the ultimate hope that our people will achieve the unity which the historically fostered consciousness of separateness had denied them. The combined and not unrelated effects of ecumenism and secularism must result in schools which comprehend whole neighbourhoods regardless of creeds and social class. Such schools could achieve that awareness of a 'fellowship in freedom' which Wolfe Tone so earnestly desired for the Irish people.

From the year 1926, when the first Report of the newly established Department of Education appeared, teachers and anyone interested in education had become accustomed to the stodgy, almost impenetrable prose in which such official documents were written. (They bear comparison in their awfulness with the prose essays by O'Farrell which at that time formed part of the compulsory course in English for the Leaving Certificate.) When, in 1962, the Report of the Council of Education appeared, it was inevitable that it, too, was leaden. It was, however, the content and not the style which Cathcart exhaustively analysed in an interview published in *The Irish Times*.

His analysis was solidly based on his understanding of the economic realities which had combined to make education an investment of first importance. He criticized the defeatist attitude revealed in a Report which could assert that 'secondary education for all' was not feasible educationally. In questioning that assumption he went on to define 'secondary education for all as a right and post-primary education as a form which could mean technical, vocational, or other non-academic forms of secondary education'.

He must have given grave offence to the conservationists with his contention that Latin and Irish had to make way for science and modern languages, and that only by a great expansion of technical education would it be possible to make efficient use of our natural resources. His expressed belief that 'the excessive emphasis on the revival of the Irish language is one which has perverted the work of our schools for long enough' was echoed by many who must have despaired that anyone would ever dare to reject that particular 'sacred cow'.

If it was as an educationist that he won widespread recognition, it is as a historian that he contributed to ending the exclusivist view of Irish nationality. And if, today, the thrust of history teaching in the Republic and in Northern Ireland alike is to create understanding and sympathy, then he can claim a share of the credit. It is now almost a quarter of a century since, as headmaster of Sandford Park, he linked History with Biology as fundamental subjects providing 'an evolutionary framework of knowledge, a perspective within which to understand the changing world'.

Cathcart, whether as headmaster or, later, as television producer, never forgot that he was first a teacher and always remained close to the thinking of teachers on matters concerning the profession. He emphasised in his public utterances the importance of giving teachers consultative rank in all decision making and he made clear the danger that lay in accepting unreservedly the views of economists and not of educationists. In a word, change was to be shaped by those in the classroom.

The many-sided nature of his activities all point to his determination to reform and, where possible, improve. Chairman of the Geography Teachers' Association, member of the Mathematics Committee of the Royal Irish Academy, chairman of Telefís Scoile, president of the Irish branch of the European Association of Teachers – he also found time to help in establishing the Joint Managerial Body which has played an important role in matters educational in the Republic.

Cathcart's close involvement in Radio Telefís Éireann and as collaborator in a number of major educational television series such as 'The Course of Irish History' led to his appointment in 1967 as Regional Director for Northern Ireland of the Independent Television Authority. Although this was an executive administrative post, he continued to produce educational television programmes such as 'Irish Landscapes' for RTE, and various school series, including 'You, Your Child and His Future', for UTV.

It is not an exaggeration to say that his work for broadcasting in Ulster has altered the perspective of thousands of schoolgoers and probably an equal number of adults. Many of the programmes that he produced, such as 'Let's Look at

Ulster', were prompted by the suggestion of teachers that they might assist in the development of environmental studies in primary and secondary schools. The attraction of such a task from his point of view was that it enabled him to provide schools with a series which was effectively an introduction to *Irish* history and *Irish* geography.

He rightly believed that if children were alerted to the historical and geographical characteristics of their neighbourhoods they would develop not only a knowledge of their heritage but a pride in it. He was keenly aware of what populist history and folklore had bred not alone in Ulster but in all parts of Ireland, and he hoped that television might through stimulating environmental studies provide young people with a more objective and less divisive approach to the past.

Script-writer as well as producer, he enjoyed a great deal of freedom, and no one can fail to remark that in his determination to achieve balance with the series 'Let's Look at Ulster' he chose Bernadette Devlin's Cookstown as a town study to complement Ian Paisley's Ballymena!

In 1972 he returned to education as professor at the New University of Ulster. Five years later he accepted a chair in education and the headship of the Department of Further Professional Studies in Education at the Queen's University of Belfast, where he still remains.

RUARC GAHAN

b. Mount Temple, County Westmeath, 1926
School: St Columba's College, Rathfarnham
University: Trinity College, Dublin
Graduated in Modern Languages, 1948
Teaching in Vocational School, Ballyfermot, Dublin

There were never very many schools in Ireland organized on any but the most conventional lines. It could hardly be otherwise in a country where a non-denominational school reflecting ordinary population distribution would have well over 90 per cent of its pupils Catholics.

When in 1957 Ruarc Gahan was appointed headmaster of Sutton Park School in Dublin, it was widely thought to be a Protestant school though it was non-denominational and had a Jew and a Catholic on its board of directors. Gahan remained there for fifteen years and in that time proved himself a teacher of courage and imagination. He always strikes me as totally logical and utterly unimpressed by the conflicting claims of Catholic and Protestant to be the sole temples of truth. Neither sect had succeeded in making Ireland a Christian country and Gahan, though not subscribing to the tenets of Christianity, has always emphasized what are considered to be Christian virtues in his teaching.

To that end, he banned corporal punishment, laid stress on humility and insisted on the dignity of each pupil as an individual. His disdain for the traditional disciplinary trappings of secondary schools did not endear him to the educational establishment, but Sutton Park, under his guidance, did become a lively, innovative, happy school.

Ruarc Gahan

Yet, despite its growth from a school of a couple of dozen boys and girls to one of two hundred and thirty by 1972, the Department of Education was no more sympathetic than it was to any school that did not observe the letter of the 'Rules and Programme'. When he put forward the case for making Sutton Park a community school, he was told that there was no demand for such a school. When he sought to arrange an exchange of pupils and teacher with a French school, his request was treated as though he was preparing to invite Martians to Ireland.

To appreciate the thinking which informed all Gahan's work, I propose to quote his own words on what he considers to be some of the underlying causes of educational discontent:

> In an unequal society the rich will be able to buy their children into private havens of sexism, elitism and religious bias, but all State-aided schools should be mixed, free and secular. They should not foster the competitive ethos: to do so is to reward greed, envy and ultimately violence. It is to sacrifice moral growth to economic growth – an evil god.
>
> Cutbacks don't matter. They might help us to return to the small and the simple: just people, with tongues, eyes, ears and perhaps writing tools. If cutbacks mean fewer remedial teachers, we might have to consider how society could cut back on the production of problem children and problem parents.
>
> Instead of labouring the obvious and discussing non-issues, then, I shall consider how the schools could confront two extremely (de)pressing problems: the failure of democracy and population growth.

THE FAILURE OF DEMOCRACY

Injustice, oppression and violence are endemic in our democracies. Gross inequality persists, power belongs to those able to buy it; electorates have little understanding of basic political concepts and little experience of challenging the assumptions that underlie them.

The schools use intimidation and authoritarian concepts to contain their students, reinforcing all that is already wrong in their lives. Every day there are confrontations, shouting, threats, verbal abuse and (despite the law) physical violence or the fear of it. School 'discipline' must soon collapse. Teachers face an intractable situation: many of their students should not have been born. They were unwanted, supernumerary, born to couples unprepared or unfitted for parenthood. They have suffered irreparable emotional damage, the behavioural effects of which might be palliated by a good one-to-one relationship with a caring adult: the classroom teacher cannot provide this.

Democracy should be practised in school, not just talked about. Pupils should be free individually and collectively to make decisions affecting their lives in school. They should be required to think, choose, accept responsibility for the results, think again and choose again. Those holding aloof from the decision-making processes (and consensus should be explored as a process) must learn to live with the decisions of those who participated. All must learn to accept responsibility for what happens in school, and, later, in the country, they must consider and discuss what sort of school they want and what sort of country they want. They must be encouraged to participate in (decentralized) democratic processes after leaving school by joining a political party or other group, or by starting their own; by sharing in the choosing of election candidates or standing for election themselves.

POPULATION GROWTH

There are already so many humans to feed, house and heat that the earth is being destroyed. We pollute the air burning non-renewable fuels, destroy soil and damage our health with artificial fertilizers and pesticides. We bury thousands of acres of fertile soil under housing estates, industrial estates and motorways. We produce too many humans and then talk of 'creating' jobs to give them 'dignity' and to delay the total breakdown of a social order that now seems inevitable.

The schools must help to create awareness of the national and world population crisis. They must challenge the dangerous notion that it's a person's own business how many babies he produces, when it's obviously everybody's business, since no person is an island. At present the schools are merely helping to contain the social crisis created by over-prolific parents by incarcerating their children for a part of each day: the teachers are bailing out a society that tolerates, even encourages, irresponsible breeding.

In Ireland we still have a country that is *relatively* unpolluted: only by achieving a population that is small, balanced and stable can we keep it so. Population studies must be an essential part of the school curriculum; sex education must distinguish between sex and procreation; no child should be let loose upon society without full information about conception and contraception.

The strength of his convictions is shown in what he has written on the cruelty and exploitation of animals that accompany food production and scientific research. In what he describes as 'The Speciesist Conspiracy', he wrote:

> Of our fellow-creatures Jeremy Bentham long ago said, 'The question is not, Can they *reason*? nor, Can they *talk*? but, *Can they suffer*?' (In Ireland today we might still add that the question is not, Have they souls?) We know that other animals can suffer, physically and mentally. And they are suffering, horribly, in vaster numbers than ever before, in our laboratories and our intensive food production units.
>
> But the schools tell nothing of this. Instead of reversing the desensitizing proces begun when parents accustom their children to eat the lambs they saw frisking on the hillside, schools reinforce it in the laboratory dissection class and in the anthropocentricity of the Christian religion that they promote in the so-called religion education class. They do not tell their pupils that animals were tortured and killed in laboratories before the cigarettes they smoke, the drugs and cosmetics they use, were put in the shops; that millions of laboratory animals go through daily hell to test new pharmaceutical products and advance the careers of scientists; that the life of the battery hen and the battery pig make bacon and egg one of the cruellest meals on earth; that millions of cows and their calves endure misery so that we can have milk in our tea; that hundreds of acres of tropical forest (homes of many creatures and lungs of the world) are destroyed daily so that the burger kings may grow feed for 'food' animals to satisfy the greed of the affluent; that the habitats of

species other than ours are being destroyed to the extent that one species disappears *for ever* each day while others struggle for survival under increasing pressure as human kind proliferates madly.

Our right to use other creatures for research, food and entertainment has been widely challenged in university departments of philosophy and by millions of persons who have disclaimed that right and gladly foregone any benefits to themselves that might accrue from it. But the schools remain relentlessly anthropocentric: it is still deemed axiomatic that the other animals were 'put there for our use' – a naïve, superstitious and cruel premiss. It is time that the schools discovered the concept of speciesism (roughly analogous to racism, sexism, ageism) and began to eliminate it from textbooks, syllabuses and the teaching of them. 'Just as we have progressed beyond the blatantly racist ethic of the era of slavery and colonialism', writes Professor Peter Singer, 'so we must now progress beyond the speciesist ethic of the era of factory farming, of the use of animals as mere research tools, of whaling, seal hunting, kangaroo slaughter and the destruction of the wilderness. We must take the final step in expanding the circle of ethics.'

Many people think of gahon as a man 'before his time'. With that I do not agree. He was and is fully aware of the needs of society. It is no accident that he made Sutton Park co-educational and non-denominational. Reformers and innovators have always to go 'too far' so that others will move forward. Gahan moved far. He also helped greatly to move others. In that lay his not inconsiderable contribution to twentieth-century Ireland.

EDWARD M. WALSH

b. Cork, 1939
School: Christian College, Cork
University: University College, Cork
Graduated in Electrical Engineering, 1961
Doctorate in Nuclear Engineering, Iowa, 1964
Director, NIHE, Limerick

A little over a quarter of a century ago the people of Limerick set up the Limerick University Project Committee. The aim of the committee was the simple if slightly ingenuous one of establishing a university college in that city.

Meetings were held, resolutions passed, deputations sent and received – to little purpose. Then, to the joy of those who knew little of Departmental ways, the Commission on Higher Education was set up. More meetings, more resolutions, more deputations. Years passed by, seven in all, before the Commission reported in 1967. It contained little of comfort to Limerick, or so it was thought at the time.

However, it did contain within it the promise of an Institute of Education for Limerick. In January 1969 Edward Walsh arrived back from the USA to take up his appointment as Director of the Institute, which opened in 1972.* He was soon to prove that those who chose him had chosen well. There were of course obstacles to be overcome and he made no secret of his dislike of the Departmental fetters that had for long placed restraints on almost all educational advance that had not the sanction of Hume Street, 'that Edwardian structure housed in a Georgian building'.

He received many invitations to speak on educational matters and his very decided views were expressed in a very decisive manner. Few who listened to him went away without new insights on old problems. Segregation in education was one of his early targets and at a conference of The European Association of Teachers in 1971 he attacked it:

> While barriers have been breached to varying extents, the evidence of segregation by social standing, segregation by religion, and segregation by sex remains. Not only are many of our students segregated within these categories but so are our teachers.

At the same conference he expresed ideas for the development of education which showed his concern for individuals rather than institutions:

> We believe that the student of the future will demand flexibility, not only because each student is an individual and consequently can benefit from an individual programme of study, but also because the student of the future, rather than receiving an education during a compacted period of time, will wish to spread that education over a significant period.

---

*The site of the National Institute of Higher Education is at Plassey on the banks of the Shannon. This was once known as Ballykilty, 'the town of the woodlands', but was changed to its present name when one of the Maunsell family who lived there shared in the triumph of Clive at the battle of Plassey during the Indian campaign of 1757. In the nineteenth century the estate passed out of the hands of the Maunsells and the last private owner was Mr Patrick Keating, who had been in the colonial service in China before coming to reside at Plassey in 1933.

Edward M. Walsh

His dislike of the 'trial by ordeal' type of examination led him to favour continuous assessment of each student and to introduce a system whereby all diploma and degree programmes at the Institute contain a period of off-campus experience. This credit system lessens the importance and, incidentally, the stress of the final examination since the candidate's success is not dependent solely on it. As the assessment records are stored on the computer, both staff and students are able to monitor progress, term by term. If in this respect he was but doing what had already been done elsewhere, he was almost certainly the first director of a third-level college to recommend the extension of the academic year to three hundred days and to make available certain facilities in the Institute on a twenty-four-hour basis.

There are today three constituent colleges forming part of the Institute: Engineering and Science, Business, and Humanities, while programmes of study are available to degree, master and doctorate level. In addition there is what is called an Innovation Centre where things happen! Someone may come there with a technology-based idea to have the resultant product evaluated, and someone may also come in search of such a product.

In a country where 'decentralization' is a theme popular with political parties when *not* in office, the NIHE in Limerick has developed a resource area of five-hundred acres away from the city of Dublin. This has already attracted technological investment from abroad as well as providing research facilities for Irish business and industry. A high degree of flexibility enables organizations of very varied interests to exist within the framework of the Institute and share in any work sanctioned by the board of directors. This close relationship with business and industry is firmly based on its co-operative education programme, which means that students also work in areas relevant to their academic interests while pursuing their studies at the Institute.

Many of Walsh's expressed ideas must have seemed strange to the staid officials of the Department. They were never uttered on impulse but derived from his analysis of needs and an estimate of resources. He had the ability, not all that common, to stand back and assess a problem before propounding a solution. Addressing Convocation of the National University of Ireland in 1984, he drew attention to the imbalance in financing higher education. Much money was, he said, being spent on the higher education of those who, because of their qualifications, were destined to become high salary earners. He favoured student loans, repayment of which was to be linked to income tax, arguing that 'those with high incomes will contribute more and compensate for those who, for one reason or another, may not have taxable income'.

Graduates of the NIHE in Limerick are as yet few. The range of courses is still being extended. Faculty is becoming stabilized and the physical surroundings are gradually giving to students the confidence that comes from an environment comparable to that of the older universities. To be a student in the largest and greatest educational investment project in the country is something to be proud of, and school-leavers are showing their awareness of its attraction by applying in increasing numbers to the Shannonside Institute.

The long-term prospects of such an institution are to some extent dependent on economic growth even more than on educational factors. The initial aim of the director has been achieved. He has given shape to an educational centre and laid down guidelines for its future advance. And, as 1845 and 1911 remain significant dates in the history of higher education, so, too, 1972 may be looked back on a century hence.

Appendix B

FOUR SCHOOLS OF DISTINCTION

IRELAND OF THE PAST had schools which were the glory of the known world. The Ireland of modern times has also its schools of unusual distinction of which I am choosing four which seem to me to owe much to their founders.

Of those I mention, I had heard something of Coláiste Éanna and Scoil Íta when growing up and, indeed, must often have seen Mary and Annie MacSwiney praying outside Cork Gaol during the hunger-strikes of the 1919-21 period. Yet it is of Mount St Benedict that I know most both from my brother-in-law, Sam Morris, who was at school there, and from John Bithrey, who taught there.

Mount St Benedict

In its short life of twenty years this school occupied two different sites. The first site chosen was at Ballinapierce, Enniscorthy, and there in September 1905 Father John Sweetman welcomed the first pupils. As numbers increased the building proved too small and in 1909 the school was moved to an imposing site near Gorey, County Wexford. Money for the purchase of the estate was mainly provided by John Sweetman of Drumbaragh, County Meath, a cousin of Father Sweetman's and a founder member of Sinn Féin.

The school brochure of 1910 states that 'In the Senior School boys are prepared for the Universities, and also for all professional examinations – Solicitor's Entrance, Woolwich, Sandhurst, etc. (Boys are not prepared for the Intermediate Examinations except at the special request of their parents.)' These were the junior, middle and senior grade examinations of the old Intermediate Education Board. While the brochure does mention facilities for 'ordinary school games', there is little evidence that anything other than cricket was ever played with enthusiasm. The list of fixtures for the School Eleven in the years before the First World War recall a lost era: Johnstown Castle, Wexford; Mount Juliet, Kilkenny; Hall Dare, Newtownbarry (now Bunclody); Coolattin, Ferns; Kynochs, Arklow.

School fees for senior pupils were £30 per term and for junior pupils £25. Without any endowment and without the Result Fees earned in schools recognized by the Intermediate Education (Ireland) Board, Mount St Benedict relied heavily on the produce of the extensive farm attached to it. The boys snared rabbits which they were allowed to cook, they fished the Slaney where it flowed near the grounds, and cut a tree for firewood only when they planted ten young trees in its place. They worked at re-stocking of streams and rivers and the planting of tobacco, as well as sheep-rearing and poultry-keeping.

It was a life in which purposeful study was linked with an awareness of the natural life around, where debate and discussion often went on unchecked after 'lights out' and where youthful minds drew inspiration from pageants and plays.

The story of the last years of the school is an unhappy one. Having incurred the episcopal wrath of Dr Codd, the Catholic Bishop of Ferns, who seemed ready to believe mischievous rumours that the headmaster harboured members of the IRA, a lengthy correspondence ensued between Dr Codd, Dom Sweetman and the Abbot of Downside. Dom Sweetman had never concealed his sympathy for Sinn Féin and when Roger Sweetman, a son of John Sweetman of Drumbaragh, stood as the Sinn Féin candidate for Wexford in the 1918 general election, Dom Sweetman appeared on his platform. He had, however, always acted within the law.

The dispute was raised at Cabinet level in 1921 at a time when Dom Sweetman was in Rome seeking Papal support in defence of the school. The Minister for Foreign Affairs, Count Plunkett, favoured the introduction of the Benedictines from Maredsous in Belgium on the grounds that they would bring new ideas and develop 'practical methods of teaching and training in use among the hard-headed Belgians'. Seán Ó Ceallaigh, the Minister for Irish, would have none of this and in his letter to the Secretary of the Cabinet, he wrote 'Níl ord iasachta aca siúd go léir ná díbreoinn nó ná coimeádfainn fé chois pé deagh-Gaedheal a bhíonn orra, fiú na Capuisínigh féin.'*

The forces opposing him proved too strong and the school closed in 1925. Twenty-eight years later Dom Sweetman died and the headmaster who had once given a school holiday in honour of the visit of King George V and Queen Mary to Dublin in 1911 was taken to his last resting-place in a coffin draped with the tricolour.

---

*Cabinet D. E. 2 - 54

The full story of 'the Mount' remains to be told. The documents, letters and episcopal decrees are contained in the 'Hollyfort file' in care of the monks of Glenstal.

Tarbert

Of the multitude of teachers who in every century was given the task of safe-guarding much of the knowledge of the past and transmitting it to later generations, how very few names have come down to us. It is true to say that memory is likely to be far more tenacious in the country, where the teacher's tricks of speech and habits, dress and interests are commented on more frequently than would be the case in the city.

Yet even in the country, few names are remembered from among those who taught my generation of school-goers. It may be that the depressingly low state of education in the 'thirties made it a period to be forgotten. The lay teacher had little status, governments seemed powerless when they were not indifferent, and only the Catholic Church was triumphant. Father Timothy Corcoran, the Jesuit Professor of Education in University College, Dublin, could boast that only six Catholic secondary schools in the country were outside the Church control.

It was against this background that Jane Agnes McKenna, a graduate of the National University, opened her school first at Glin, County Limerick, and later at Tarbert where she was to spend her teaching life.

I first heard of her school when in France! I was taking a French course at Tours and one of the Irish teachers staying in the university hostel spoke enthusiastically of what one woman was doing in a remote part of north Kerry.

I never saw the school which was burned down some years later but it lives in the hearts of its pupils in a way that schools rarely do. One of her pupils, Brendan Kennelly, describes it as 'a big house, yellow-painted at the top of a hilly field' and that gives it an identity as sharp as Haworth Parsonage to those familiar with simple country scenes.

The school she founded in the early 1940s scorned the factory system whereby doors opened at 9 o'clock in the morning and closed usually at some time between 3 o'clock and 4 o'clock in the afternoon. If preparing a play or enjoying a poem or seeking the solution to a problem held the interest of the pupils beyond the hours of class, then that was considered as a good reason as any for staying on. Often it was the need to return home to help with the milking or in autumn with the lifting of the potato crop that brought a reluctant end to the school-day.

And what a full day it was for those children to whom the treasures of literature, of art and of distant lands were revealed as their imagination carried them far beyond the gentle hills that lay between them and the Shannon. The school was their second home and they were encouraged to stay and read in the book-filled rooms and, as they grew older, to return in the evening to study a foreign language, listen to music or, simply, to talk.

The shadow of the certificate examinations did not appear to have darkened their days as it did elsewhere. They were prepared for them by Patrick and Alice Carey, by Miss McKenna herself and by Mrs Enright. Competition was never stressed and so they came to regard each examination as an exercise in self-measurement. What their teaching taught them above all else was to discover their own abilities, to consider them objectively, and to develop as best they could their individual qualities.

The pupils at Tarbert were almost certainly less overtly

nationalistic than those at Pearse's school in Rathfarnham, a school with which it bears comparison, but love of country was implicit in the life of the yellow house on the hill.

The school gave them a new pride in their birthplace, a sense of the past firmly anchored in values that they understood. It was at the core of so much that went on in the parish that it lent a greater cohesiveness to the life of that small rural community. A regard for learning was traditional: it took on a new meaning for many boys and girls as they read and listened and sang and acted. An interest in sport was deep-rooted: it grew as they played together and later watched classmates attain to the glory of the green and gold jersey.

With fees, when they were charged, as low as £9 a year, she cannot have made money. Neither of course did Pearse. Their work continued without benefit of cost accountants or school bursars. They shared with their pupils the riches of the mind. And the real wealth of Tarbert lay in the pupils who went out into the world carrying something of the vision and the dreams of Jane Agnes McKenna.

Scoil Íte

'As I hold education to be primarily a spiritual question and as the education of the country from a national point of view is based on falsehood and dishonesty, the resultant deterioration of our land in nationality and in honesty and in all spiritual values is an accusation in itself of the system of education in Ireland.' The words are contained in a letter to me, dated 27 December 1952, from one of the co-founders of Scoil Íte in Cork, Eithne MacSwiney. Her sister, Mary, had died nine years earlier and it was not until the summer of 1954 that Eithne, in the face of increasing ill-health, took down the name-plate and finally closed the school.

Ever since that September day in 1916 when the school opened, the two sisters had aimed to inspire the pupils with 'a love for, a loyalty to, and a pride in the heritage of their land'. The people not only of Cork but from far outside the city gave their support to the school wherein children were taught not alone to value what was best in the culture of their own land but also in that of other countries.

Traditionally, Cork people sent their daughters to the nuns. Lay teachers were, it was felt, less suited to positions of authority and could adequately exercise their profession in some subordinate capacity. A certain cachet applied to an education in one of the upper class convents of which there were then at least two in Cork city. Nor did the government offer much in the way of encouragement. Grants for building and maintenance did not exist and schools with large numbers and a high rate of examination success alone could hope to prosper.

The two sisters who had received their teacher-training in England, Mary in Cambridge and Eithne in the Isle of Wight, set very high standards. The classics as well as modern languages formed part of the curriculum, and music as well as painting were given an importance unknown in most second-level schools. But it was the ethos of the school that has left the most enduring impression on the past pupils to whom I have spoken. Honesty, integrity and self-respect were the qualities which were most emphasized and which gave to the school a prestige out of all proportion to its size. My mother, whose sympathies were never with the Republican movement, always held Mary and Eithne MacSwiney in very high regard.

If, as has often been said, the quality of mind of the

teacher is what matters most in education, then the pupils were especially fortunate. Among those who taught there either in a whole-time or part-time capacity were François Lefèvre, Louise O'Leary and Germaine Stockley. While it was a single-sex school, boys were accepted in the junior department up to the age of ten and it must have been one of the first schools in the country to introduce supervised study after school hours.

Though the school was within a few hundred yards of my home on Wellington Road, I visited it but once. It was the family home of the MacSwineys and what impressed me most was the care taken with the furnishing of the classrooms. Good reproductions of paintings on the walls and in the corridors, solid comfortable desks in the classrooms, and carpets, so good for muffling sound, everywhere. And it is well to remember that even after the departure of the British from part of the country, Scoil Íte never recognized the Irish Free State and so did not qualify for any government grants.

It had the recognition that mattered most – the love and affection of those who look back to the formative years spent in 4 Belgrave Place, Cork.

Newtown

Arnold Marsh who died in 1977, was one of the great headmasters. During his teaching life he was associated with three splendid Quaker foundations, Lisburn, Newtown (Waterford) and Drogheda. His work as headmaster in Newtown and Drogheda enabled him to put into effect some of his entirely practical views on education. Yet education occupied but part of a life lived at many levels and in many lands.

He was born in Belfast but much of his school life was spent in Somerset and he was almost thirty before he settled permanently in Ireland. The intervening years had been spent in places as far distant as British Colombia and Alaska, working at a variety of jobs.

When in 1926 he came as a headmaster to Newtown, his career may be said to have taken definite shape. Newtown is a school where independence of thought is encouraged, where work, whether mental or physical, is valued for its own sake and where pupils are taught that social justice and peace are always worth striving for.

Newtown was known for the manual and artistic skills of its pupils long before an academic-minded Department of Education came to recognize the importance of woodwork and metalwork, painting and music. To anyone educated at the school, such subjects were never considered 'out-of-school' activities. As one of those closely connected with Newtown, John Brigham, wrote in his pamphlet 'Aspects of Education', 'Culture is not only of the brain or the brush; it may be a solid, back-breaking hobby like gardening, or work with a reconstruction corps.'

Newtown School is today a school of approaching three hundred pupils, far different from the rather run-down building with its twenty pupils which Marsh took over on 1 January 1926. If in appearance it has changed, the enduring values of the Religious Society of Friends who founded it have not. And, if it now attracts pupils of all denominations, the independent spirit and determined goodwill of the old Quakers are still very much part of the school. The values it seeks to inculcate in its pupils are timeless, and Newtown School has cherished them for close on two hundred years.